Metropolitan Detroit: An Anatomy of Social Change

Robert Sinclair
and
Bryan Thompson
Wayne State University

Ballinger Publishing Company • Cambridge, Massachusetts
A Subsidiary of J.B. Lippincott Company

This book is printed on recycled paper.

International Standard Book Number: 0-88410-469-9

Library of Congress Catalog Card Number: 76-48300

Printed in the United States of America

Library of Congress Cataloging in Publication Data

Sinclair, Robert, 1930–
  Metropolitan Detroit.

  Bibliography: p.
  1. Detroit metropolitan area—Social conditions. 2. Detroit metropolitan area—Economic conditions. 3. Anthropo-geography—Detroit metropolitan area. I. Thompson, Bryan, joint author. II. Title.
  HN80.D6S54   309.1'774'3404   76-48300
  ISBN 0-88410-469-9

Contents

List of Figures

List of Tables

Acknowledgements

Many persons have provided assistance in the preparation of this study. The authors have been dependent upon the willing help of individuals in many agencies, upon the secretarial efforts of a few stalwarts during the days of final preparation, and most particularly upon the field work and suggestions of a large number of Wayne geography students during the development of the work. In particular, the authors acknowledge the expertise and assistance of Helen Willis in the Oakland Township study, of David Hartman in the Cass Corridor study, and of Paul Travalini in various phases of the work. Cartographers Larry Banka, Nick Rea, and Steve Abbey provided not only their skills, but also creative suggestions when needed. The Northwest Detroit study is a modified version of an article by R. Sinclair in the *Wiener Geographische Schriften, Festschrift Leopold G. Scheidl,* vol. 2 (1975).

Introduction to the Detroit System

The sprawling Detroit metropolitan complex of 4.2 million people forms the nation's fifth largest urban agglomeration. The city of Detroit, with about a million and a half inhabitants, lies at the heart of the system. Over eighty independent incorporated political units surround the city, nine of them with populations approaching or exceeding 100,000 (Figure 1). Suburban expansion has been rapid during the last three decades, such that the suburban population surpassed that of Detroit during the fifties, and by 1970, within the Standard Metropolitan Statistical Area alone, was 1.8 times that of Detroit.

Growth in the region has fanned out northward away from the Detroit River "hinge line" in an ever widening radius that consumes increasing segments of southeastern Michigan. Much of the development has been along a flat glacial lake plain, with the landscape becoming more rolling in the morainic belt to the northwest. Superimposed over the landscape are wide arteries and expressways that appear to stretch endlessly in all directions. Single family homes on tree-lined streets typify most parts of the region.

Detroit is a workingman's town, dominated by the automobile industry. Historically, the industry has been influential in shaping the region's growth, as industrial development jumped ahead of the built-up area, and then pulled the edge of urbanization toward it. Visitors and newcomers quickly learn that Detroit is the heartland of the American labor movement, with union activities that have na-

tionwide repercussions. The presence of the auto industry permeates all facets of life in Detroit, whether it be driving along the Chrysler Freeway, listening to a concert in Ford Auditorium, watching the construction of the Walter P. Reuther Library on the Wayne State University campus, or supporting Detroit's professional basketball team, appropriately called the Pistons.

A sameness, monotony, and lack of sophistication pervades much of Detroit's life, suggesting that auto industry principles have spilled over into many walks of life. At the same time, Detroit projects a sense of power, a dynamism, and an ability to get things done, as was illustrated after Pearl Harbor when the auto industry rapidly adapted to become the main armament supplier for the national war effort.

Detroit is one of the nation's leading black cities, and much of the social change of the last two decades is the result of the rapid increase in the size of the black community. This accelerated growth was initiated by the war time and postwar industrial expansion of the 1940s, which in turn led to large scale immigration from the South. The presence, power, and influence of Detroit's black population helped elect Coleman Young, the city's first black mayor. Many of the country's black literary, artistic, and musical leaders either are based in Detroit or began careers there. A large proportion of the city's commercial establishments, places of entertainment, and recreational events cater to the black culture. However, the

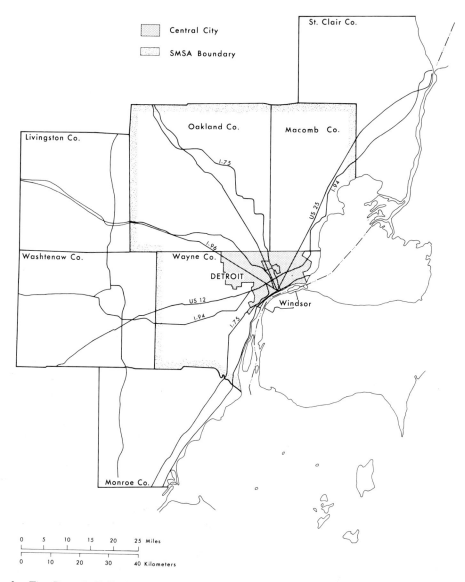

Figure 1. The Detroit Daily Urban System. All counties included send daily commuters to jobs in Detroit and Wayne County.

black presence in the central city contrasts markedly with its complete absence in most suburban communities.

Throughout its history Detroit has projected an image, a dream, a hope, and a promise to millions of unskilled workers. For many, those promises were fulfilled, the factories providing a springboard into the middle class for many of their children and grandchildren. For others the reality was disappointment, deprivation, conflict, and despair. The hopes and

images are still alive today, but so are the tensions, fears, and struggles.

Detroit today projects a negative national image. Memories of the 1967 riot—the most severe and violent disturbance in recent American history—are still vivid. The city has recently achieved the dubious distinction of being the nation's homicide capital. Other alarming statistics stand out clearly—for example, fully one-quarter of the nation's abandoned HUD-owned homes are in Detroit. These images have some basis in fact. Crime and fear of crime are widespread. Protective devices, burglar alarm systems, "Beware of Dog" signs, and a swelling army of security guards have become an accepted aspect of the city's landscape. Urban decay is widespread. Many formerly prosperous commercial strips along major arteries now are characterized by vacant or boarded-up stores. Residential blight marks many neighborhoods.

The negative image, however, is misleading if applied indiscriminately. For the Detroit area also boasts attractive residential areas unsurpassed in the country. Throughout the suburban area are new and attractive shopping malls, with no apparent dearth of customers. The metropolitan area as a whole offers a wealth of outdoor recreational amenities, particularly for water-based activities. The central city itself has many quiet, tree-lined residential areas, viable ethnic communities, and highly reputed cultural and civic centers.

The Detroit area presents many faces. It is an urban region of sharp contrasts and extremes. Nevertheless, Detroit does epitomize the ills of American urban society in the mid-1970s and it might well be that our society's future depends upon how Detroit and cities like it approach, handle, and resolve what in many respects are similar problems.

This study is intended to capture the mood and the character of the metropolitan area; to complement, as well as to add to, the insights and descriptions obtained from an analysis of census data. Three themes are incorporated. The first portrays the metropolis as a mosaic of six contrasting social realms, highly interdependent but separated both by social distance and by different outlooks.

The second theme describes how the social realms of the Detroit system are engulfed by a series of external changes, including such forces as urban expansion, commercial and industrial relocation, urban renewal, expressway construction, and racial change. These forces of change and the instability they provide not only impinge upon the system, they have become an essential part of the system.

The third theme considers those forces at a more local level, recognizing that all parts of the Detroit system are not affected in the same way. This section examines, in specific areas, the chain of events set in motion by those forces and their effects both on the physical landscape and on people's lives. Three examples are chosen as representative of the important forces of change operating in different parts of the Detroit system. These are (1) an inner city community whose very survival is threatened by institutional growth, (2) a section of northwest Detroit undergoing racial change, and (3) an outlying semirural township threatened by urban sprawl.

In essence, the study is social in perspective. It analyzes the characteristics of and processes operating in basic segments of the Detroit area's social structure. It focuses upon the nature of several dominant forces of spatial change. Finally, it examines the landscape changes, and individual responses that occur as spatial change forces engulf selected parts of the system.

The Detroit System and its Regions

A SPATIAL MODEL OF THE DETROIT AREA

The Detroit system evolved as a complex mosaic of areas, each with distinctive social, economic, and physical characteristics. At first glance this mosaic appears to have little or no order or structure. What interrelationships may exist are obscured by the apparently chaotic assemblage of outlooks, lifestyles and social makeup. A spatial model is proposed to facilitate the conceptualization of the Detroit area and to provide a framework for analyzing the processes operating in the area (Figure 2).

The model divides the Detroit system into six zones. Economically, these six zones are interdependent and interacting, each performing a vital function in the total operation of the Detroit system's economy. For example, the assembly lines of the Suburban Area of Intersectoral Development are manned largely by workers from the Detroit Middle Zone. The administrative and financial offices of the Detroit Inner Zone are the work places of executives whose homes and social lives are to be found in the Suburban Area of Radial Development. Those same homes are cleaned and serviced by maids and cleaning personnel who reverse commute from Detroit's Inner and Middle Zones.

Ironically, the functional interdependence of the different zones exists alongside a condition of strict social segregation. For despite interdependent contractual relationships, residents of one zone have little social contact with those of other zones. The assembly workers who swarm to the automobile factories of the Suburban Area of Intersectoral Development return to the Detroit Middle Zone whenever the shift is over. They hardly understand, let alone participate in, the social life of their areas of employment. The women who provide maid services in the Suburban Area of Radial Development likewise return to the Detroit Inner and Middle Zones when their daily chores are performed. The executives who commute daily from this Radial Zone to the administrative offices of the Detroit Inner Zone are effectively screened from the realities of life in that zone.

The essential dichotomy between a functional and contractual interdependence of the different zones on the one hand, and a strict interzonal segregation and ignorance on the other, is an important theme of this chapter. The way in which this zonal pattern has evolved has been analyzed by Sinclair in *The Face of Detroit*. It is the concern of the present chapter to describe the zones themselves. Each zone is treated separately, starting with the Detroit Inner Zone and finishing with the Zone of Rural Change.

THE DETROIT INNER ZONE

The Inner Zone forms the hub of the Detroit system. It is a zone of contrasts, with powerful and sound business, commercial, and institutional interests juxtaposed with elements of

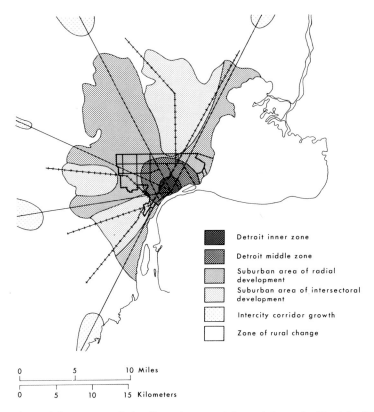

Figure 2. The six activity zones of the Detroit area. Adapted from R. Sinclair, *The Face of Detroit.* (Detroit: Wayne State University–National Council for Geographic Education–U.S. Office of Education, 1970).

society that are unwanted, discarded, or simply left behind in the wake of rapid change. The overwhelming visual impressions are those of a central business district that is not what it used to be, of large and expanding public institutions, of submerged expressways that carve the area into small parcels, of decay and poverty, of vast wasteland tracts where homes once stood, and of piecemeal residential development that has sprung up in the wake of urban renewal. Feelings in the zone are highly divergent. On the one hand are the poor—suspicious, angry, frustrated, and relatively powerless as they witness their communities decay or being bulldozed out of existence. At the other extreme are those whose hope is for revitalization, in which a new commercial, business, and institutional complex will attract a middle and upper class clientele back into the city core.

Extending about three to four miles in all directions from the downtown business cen-

ter, the Inner Zone occupies a relatively small area of the Detroit metropolitan complex (Figure 2). The zone is bounded by the Detroit River to the south and Grand Boulevard on all sides. It is crisscrossed and carved up by a network of arterials and expressways, of which Woodward Avenue, running northwest from downtown, is the main arterial street.

As the original nucleus of the Detroit region, the Inner Zone has changed with every development in the area's long history, from a Great Lakes trading center centering around Fort Pontchartrain, to a commercial center serving an expanding frontier, to a thriving manufacturing area, to the business district and central core of a great American metropolis. These changes were accompanied by dramatic advances in transportation as Detroit changed from a walking city, to a horse and buggy city, to an electric railroad and horse-drawn streetcar city, to an electric streetcar city, and finally to an automobile city.

Each of those eras has left its mark upon the housing stock of the inner city. Large old mansions are found in certain sections, the legacy of the upper class of the late nineteenth century. More modest single and two family frame houses of the same general period are concentrated near the industrial areas along the railroads. Apartment hotels, scattered among single family residential areas, reflect the surge of population in the early twentieth century. At that time crowding became more common, poor quality housing was built along alleys, and single family housing was turned into multiple unit housing. By the first decade of this century, the inner city was built up, and since then housing has been noted for its succession of occupants rather than for new developments. New construction had to await the urban renewal programs of the last two decades.

The Inner Zone served as port of entry for the thousands of unskilled workers who flocked to Detroit during the first three decades of the twentieth century. As has been traditional in most American cities, these immigrants grouped together in enclaves surrounding the central business area. Virtually every one of Detroit's major ethnic groups had its original nucleus in the Inner Zone. Germans, Italians, Jews, and blacks were at some time in their settlement history concentrated in the near east side. Poles settled north of Gratiot on the east side and near the Michigan-Junction intersection on the west side. The Irish concentrated immediately west of downtown in the area known as Corktown. These ethnic colonies have long since left the inner city, expanding in a sectoral pattern into the Detroit Middle Zone and beyond. However, some residual evidence permits the reconstruction of the social history of early reception zones. In the former Germantown, for example, names and dates can still be seen on old buildings, Stroh's Brewery has remained and expanded, restaurants like Joe Muer's and Schweizer's still are culinary landmarks, and St. Joseph's Roman Catholic Church at Jay and Orleans streets is a silent sentinel of a nostalgic past.

The economic boom of World War II and the postwar period subjected the Inner Zone to pressures similar to those of the past. Southern whites and blacks, and several new minority groups, with aspirations similar to the groups which preceded them, surged to the Inner Zone

to take the place of those who had migrated to other zones. These postwar immigrants remain as the most important residents of the Inner Zone.

The Inner Zone today is an area of contrast and extremes. A declining central business district, virtually cut off from surrounding areas by encircling expressways, remains the pivotal point. By day the downtown area bustles as white collar professionals from widely separated parts of the metropolitan area carry on their business activities. By early evening downtown becomes desolate as lawyers, office workers, and city employees return to outlying suburbs along arterial and expressway systems that literally dismember the Inner Zone. Retail stores in the central business district increasingly are being shunned, particularly by a middle class which resents the inconveniences of downtown shopping and now prefers outlying shopping malls. Nightlife is a shadow of its former self. Many movie theaters have closed, restaurants close earlier, and a walk along Woodward Avenue at 10:00 P.M. often can be an eerie, lonesome experience. A single bright and refreshing exception—Greektown—tends to accentuate the emptiness of the balance of the downtown area.

Four miles to the north is a second downtown, the New Center area, housing the world headquarters of General Motors Corporation, the world headquarters of Burroughs Corporation, and numerous other business and professional offices. The New Center likewise bustles with activity by day, but becomes empty by early evening.

A striking concentration of public institutions is found in the Inner Zone, particularly an expanding institutional complex that straddles Woodward Avenue and virtually links downtown with the New Center area. The Medical Center, immediately east of Woodward, is fast becoming one of the world's largest medical complexes, incorporating hospitals, nursing homes, professional plazas, and the Wayne State University Medical School. Immediately to the north is the Cultural Center with the International Institute, the Rackham Memorial Building, the Detroit Institute of Arts, and the Detroit Public Library. Adjacent to the Cultural Center are Wayne State University and the Merrill-Palmer Institute. Within this corridor are found the Detroit area's major theaters for the performing arts, including the Ford Auditorium, the Masonic Temple, the Fisher Theater, and Wayne State University's Hilberry and Bonstelle theaters. Within the Inner Zone are sports stadia including Cobo Arena, Tiger Stadium, and Olympia, providing facilities for major league basketball, baseball, and hockey.

The recent expansion of many of these institutions has been made possible by urban renewal legislation. Urban renewal is also responsible for other developments. Immediately east of downtown, an extensive high- and low-rise middle and upper income residential development has arisen on what was Black Bottom, once the heart of the Black Ghetto. To the west of downtown, an industrial park has decimated and replaced the Corktown community.

This institutional landscape exists alongside another kind of landscape. It is a ravaged landscape, characterized by blight, by empty wastelands surrounded by white fences (the Detroit stamp of urban renewal), by overgrown, glass-littered playgrounds, and by residential pockets cut off from each other by broad expressways and urban renewal "overkill." Beer cans, trash, weeds, and broken glass comprise much of the surface material. Stores in what once were prosperous commercial strips are vacant or abandoned, as are numerous industrial and office buildings. Those few stores that remain invariably are screened by protective devices, command high prices, and generally provide inferior goods and services. Industry remaining in the zone faces problems of vandalism in aging structures no longer suited to modern production methods. The only services that appear to be thriving are Salvation Army missions, soup kitchens, and other social and welfare services.

The Inner Zone has both a resident population and a visitor population. The latter has no permanent locational commitment to the zone but comes into the zone to work, to see the Detroit Tigers or the Red Wings, to watch a Broadway play at the Fisher Theater, or to partake of the "blue entertainment" readily available in the area.

The resident population is quite different. Essentially, the Inner Zone is the domain of the poor and the downtrodden, those who are "rejected," "forgotten," or "left behind" by other elements of Detroit society. More than 25 percent of the zone's 37,000 families subsist on

incomes below the poverty level. A large proportion of the population is on welfare. Even in 1972, a relatively prosperous year, the unemployment rate for the employable population in Detroit's Model Neighborhood, located in the Inner Zone, was 16 percent, and almost 40 percent for eighteen to twenty-four year old heads of households. Large numbers of people are old, single, and immobile. About half the respondents in the Model Neighborhood area have no access to a car. Skid row and its accompanying institutions also are found here, often intermingling with and imposing themselves upon adjacent residential areas.

Of the thriving ethnic groups that were present at the turn of the century, only the Poles and the blacks remain in any great numbers, and the continued presence of a vital Polish community is an uncertain prospect. Several other ethnic groups have found a niche in the zone in more recent times. A large Mexican-American community is located along West Vernor and Bagley streets, and a small but highly nucleated Maltese community resides near Tiger Stadium. Other recent settlement has included American Indians, Appalachian whites, Indians, and Pakistanis.

The lifestyle of the poor in the Inner Zone is simple, and highly circumscribed. For most it is concerned with solving day-to-day problems. For some it is an acute struggle for survival. In some residential districts family life is strong, and there is some neighborhood identity in spite of conditions of severe poverty. For single individuals and old persons living in apartments, life tends to be a lonely and dull routine. For the skid row alcoholic, life conforms to the stereotyped pattern of day-to-day survival. For all elements, life is highly localized. Social activity is limited to the immediate blocks, the corner store, the bar, and in some communities the church. This lifestyle does not incorporate the nearby cultural and institutional amenities of the Inner Zone. It is not the typical Inner City resident who frequents the Detroit Institute of Arts, who attends the symphony concerts in Ford Auditorium, who watches sports events in Cobo Hall, and whose children are students at Wayne State University.

Quite a different lifestyle exists in the few middle and upper income enclaves in the Inner Zone, such as Indian Village or the East Lafayette area. From one viewpoint life in those enclaves is restricted and cut off from the immediate environs. Yet in other ways it is free-wheeling and highly mobile. Shopping trips are made to suburban malls, friends are scattered throughout the suburbs, recreational activities might range from frequent trips to northern Michigan to less frequent journeys that are worldwide in scope.

As it has been throughout its long and dynamic history, the Inner Zone today is subjected to sweeping forces of change. Often these forces appear to oppose and contradict one another. For example, renewal has been a dominant force, as federal urban renewal projects developed some areas and private and public institutions expanded into others. At the same time, blight encompasses ever larger areas as properties decay and services deteriorate. There is some degree of relationship between those apparently contradictory forces. Many persons displaced by construction projects, unable or unwilling to move to other parts of the metropolitan area, have crowded into adjacent residential blocks causing a more rapid rate of deterioration there. An example is the migration of skid row residents and transients from their demolished Michigan Avenue area into the Woodward, Cass, and Second Avenue districts north of the central business district. Moreover, the climate of uncertainty connected with institutional expansion has lowered the incentive for property maintenance in adjacent areas.

A second apparent contradiction is the attempt, on the one hand, to bring jobs and middle and upper income residents back to the inner city while, on the other hand, businesses and jobs are departing from the area. The much discussed riverside Renaissance Center, it is hoped, will start a trend bringing businesses, people, and life back into the downtown area. As the project was being discussed and built, the headquarters of the Kresge Corporation left its Cass Park location for suburban Troy, the Michigan Automobile Association left downtown Detroit for a new location in Dearborn, and even the *Detroit News* moved many of its main operations to Sterling Heights.

A third contradiction is that developments expected to benefit the inner city and its residents are increasingly resented and opposed by those same residents. The contradiction undoubtedly stems from the history of past renewal and redevelopment which has favored commercial, industrial, institutional, and mid-dle class interests, and tended to ignore or misunderstand the plight of local residents. The result has been a climate of suspicion and resentment surrounding virtually every institutional construction project. Unfortunately that climate remains today, at a time when official attitudes toward renewal have changed greatly and developments are subject to and dependent upon local and resident control. Often the eventual result is that vast tracts of land remain idle, and new construction is stymied as local interests and development interests seek to come to terms.

Perhaps these contradictions epitomize the Inner Zone today and explain its divergent outlooks toward the future. One outlook is that of rejuvenation and revitalization, with the premise that a new commercial-institutional-residential complex will lure business back to the Inner Zone and restore its former role as the exciting hub of the metropolitan area. The other outlook is quite different. It sees the Inner Zone as the home of thousands of families and individuals who do not have the wealth, mobility, or desire to live elsewhere. For them rejuvenation is a threat, and every incoming institution becomes a potential displacement of their homes and their community life. There would seem to be no real reason why those two divergent outlooks cannot be accommodated to create a mixed and healthy environment for all who wish to live and work in the Inner Zone. Today that accommodation appears to be hindered by a legacy of suspicion and frustration derived from the past. Meanwhile much of the Inner Zone remains in a state of limbo between what was a viable and exciting past and a somewhat vague, uncertain future.

THE DETROIT MIDDLE ZONE

The Middle Zone comprises the largest part of the city of Detroit. The zone provides much of the unskilled and semiskilled factory working force upon which the automobile industry, in the suburbs as well as in the city, depends. It has become the home of Detroit's black population. The zone has been virtually transformed by recent social change. The spread of blight and neighborhood instability associated with this change is well advanced in large areas. Whether these processes continue or can be checked might well be the key to Detroit's future.

Throughout much of the zone, the initial visual impression is one of solid single family residential neighborhoods, typified by attractive tree-lined streets. Some of these neighborhoods, particularly on the east side, are inhabited by first and second generation Eastern European immigrants and have remained stable for decades. Others have become the reception zones for new immigrants from the Middle East and the Balkans. The most typical, however, are neighborhoods which only recently have become black, or which currently are undergoing racial transition. Thus, throughout much of the zone, "for sale" signs abound on front lawns, confrontations occur in the schools, and harassment of black newcomers in white areas and of the remaining whites in black areas often occurs. This social turbulence is the breeding ground for much of Detroit's physical decay and also for its reputation for violent crime.

The Middle Zone surrounds the Inner Zone in a three mile wide semicircular belt which encompasses most of the city of Detroit (Figure 2). Only the northwest and extreme northeast sections of the city are excluded. The political enclaves of Hamtramck and Highland Park are integral parts of the zone. The zone was built during Detroit's dynamic growth period between 1900 and the early 1930s. Development typically followed the pattern of the automobile industry, which first concentrated along the New York Central, Grand Trunk, and Detroit Terminal railroads that surrounded and penetrated the central parts of the city, and later jumped to the "outlying suburbs" of Highland Park, Hamtramck, and East Dearborn. Residential districts filled in the intervening areas, while the city's commercial structure was laid out on major streets, most notably along the radial arteries (Jefferson, Gratiot, Woodward, Grand River, Michigan, and Fort) that fanned out from the inner city. To a large degree the Middle Zone, along with the Inner Zone, was the Detroit system of the pre–World War II years.

Residential growth of the Middle Zone was differentiated along ethnic and class lines. Large scale immigration led to an extension of the ethnic pattern that had been established earlier in the Inner Zone (Figure 3). Thus, prior to World War II, stable residential patterns existed.

The largest ethnic settlements were Polish, one centered in Hamtramck, the other near Michigan Avenue and Junction in West Detroit. The Italian settlement had moved northeast along Gratiot Avenue. The center of Hungarian settlement was in Delray, a heavy industrial area in southwest Detroit. English, Scots, and Jews were heavily concentrated in the northwest between Woodward and Grand River avenues. The German community, though more dispersed, had moved to the northeast along Gratiot and Harper. The black community was still confined to a narrow corridor east of Woodward Avenue.

World War II and its aftermath inaugurated a transformation of the Middle Zone that in a sense has continued to the present. Two interconnected processes were involved. One was the massive immigration of blacks, whose percentage of Detroit's total population changed from 9.3 in 1940 to 44.5 in 1970. The other was the movement to the suburbs—particularly of middle or upper income white families with school children. The fact that overall suburban movement exceeded that of the black immigration has had significant consequences for the Middle Zone. First, it has meant an overall decrease in the city's population from about 1,850,000 in the 1950s to 1,511,482 in 1970. Second, it has meant that residential areas were opened up more rapidly, so that racial transition has been more rapid and more widespread than in most other cities in the country. However, the pattern of growth of the black community has not been uniform throughout the Middle Zone. In some areas, particularly on the east side, Southern and Eastern European ethnic groups, with a strong attachment to the neighborhood, the parish, the church, and the parochial school, have remained and the black community has surrounded rather than displaced them. By contrast in the northwest side, where the English, Scottish, and Jewish populations were more mobile, racial transition has been much more rapid. Most recently, as if to emphasize that residential patterns are not that simplistic, the Inner Zone has become the initial settlement area for several new immigrant groups, particularly Albanians, Yemenis, and Iraqis.

The changes of the last two decades have had a disastrous effect upon the Middle Zone's commercial structure. The prosperous radial commercial arteries and the thriving outlying

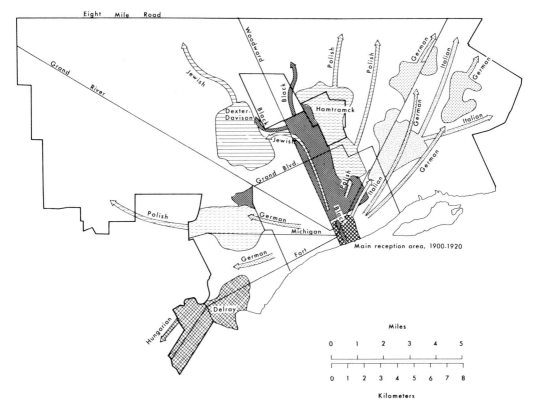

Figure 3. Detroit's ethnic communities in 1950, and major migration paths, 1900-1950.

business districts that typified Detroit's prewar and war time commercial structure have well nigh been obliterated, victims of the changing economic structure of nearby neighborhoods and the competition of suburban shopping malls. A drive along commercial arteries like Grand River and Gratiot reveals an almost uninterrupted sequence of empty stores, broken glass, boarded-up store fronts, and temporary if any occupance. Remaining businesses tend to reflect the changing socioeconomic and racial character of nearby areas. Thus, in the inner parts of the zone, stores serve a black clientele and include a high proportion of record shops, wig stores, storefront churches, barbecue restaurants, hair stylists, and party stores. Farther out businesses tend to be transitional, with large numbers of automobile showrooms, service stations, loan company offices, and real estate offices.

The industrial districts of the Middle Zone, which comprised a major part of the prewar automobile industry, have long since lost that role to the industrial corridors of the Suburban

Area of Intersectoral Development. Some districts have shells of buildings and unused facilities. Many industries that do remain occupy congested sites and structures ill-suited to modern production methods. However, several major automobile plants have remained in the Middle Zone. Dodge Main in Hamtramck, the Chrysler plant on East Jefferson, the Ford plant in Highland Park, and the Cadillac plant on Michigan Avenue are still significant units in the American automobile industry. At the same time, they employ only a part of the unskilled and semiskilled labor force of the Middle Zone. The remaining part commutes daily to the more important manufacturing employment centers in the Suburban Intersectoral Zone.

The Middle Zone houses a population that includes both middle and lower middle income blue collar and white collar workers. This population mans the assembly lines of local and suburban automobile factories, provides the civil servants for federal and local government offices, does secretarial work in downtown and local offices, performs personal services, and is engaged in social work and local teaching. Distinct differences exist between the typical black and white member of the Middle Zone. The black middle class Detroiter typically is young, married, with children and a working wife. Family income is slightly higher than the Detroit city average. His white counterpart is older, no longer has children living at home, and often is of East European descent. His family income is slightly below the average for the city. In Hamtramck, for example, 50 percent of the 1970 population was designated as foreign stock, compared to 22 percent for Detroit. Twenty-one percent of Hamtramck's population was over sixty years old, compared with 16.2 percent for the city of Detroit, and 11.9 for the metropolitan area.

These differences between the black and white populations show up in their respective life patterns. In some older white ethnic neighborhoods, life still has an old world flavor, and is slow-moving, nostalgic, and church- and community-oriented. Local markets, bakeries, ethnic food stores, bars, restaurants, and churches serve important social functions for the community and provide an important link with the past for former residents, long since moved to the suburbs, who visit the communities in which they were raised and where they still have relatives and fond memories. But there is abundant evidence that this lifestyle is on an almost inevitable decline. Even the main commercial street of Hamtramck, Joseph Campau, exhibits all the indexes of commercial blight. The extreme of decay has been reached in the Hungarian community of Delray, where deterioration is reminiscent of the worst aspects of the Detroit Inner Zone.

Life in the black community must be considered on a different scale. The Middle Zone is the source of cultural, political, and economic strength for one of the nation's leading black cities. The community has accomplished much in the last decade. Detroit's first black mayor was elected in 1973. A young generation of leaders is emerging as blacks occupy more influential positions in the city's political, economic, and cultural life. The contribution of Detroit blacks to the nation's cultural life is well known. The literature, art, theater, and music emanating from black Detroit has had a wide impact. The Motown sound remains a Detroit sound even though the company of that name has moved to the West Coast. Much of black Detroit is young, energetic, colorful, and fashionable. The church also is strong, and from its ranks have come local leaders like Reverend Nicholas Hood and Reverend Albert Cleage.

But Detroit's black community still has many long term problems. It incorporates an area that is characterized by spreading physical blight in a city plagued by deep and continuing financial difficulties. It has an unemployment rate that is higher than the metropolitan average. There is tension and mistrust between blacks and the Detroit Police Department. Discriminatory housing practices still exclude blacks from most suburbs. Increasing power at the local level means little when it can be stymied by actions at the state level. A lifestyle of increasing affluence can be frustrating if restrictions and embarrassments occur when traveling or pursuing recreational activities. To a much greater degree than their white suburban counterparts, the life patterns of middle and upper income blacks are concentrated within the limits of the Inner and Middle zones.

The Middle Zone today is subjected to forces of change which probably are more pronounced, dramatic, and visible than in any other zone. Most apparent is racial change. The zone has been a veritable case study of racial transition, with 7,000 to 9,000 housing units changing from white to black occupancy every year since 1950. The transition has been typified by contiguous "ghetto" expansion, with many of the associated symbols like rumor spreading, blockbusting, panic selling, and nefarious real estate practices. Tensions have been high in areas undergoing racial change, as has been uncertainty in areas in the path of racial change. Periodically those tensions have given rise to harassment of individuals and hostilities in schools. The instability associated with the racial change process has made many attempts at neighborhood improvement quite futile, and has dashed most hopes for stable integrated communities.

Closely associated with rapid social change is an apparently relentless spread of blight. Flight of previous homeowners, postponement of upkeep investment in the face of uncertainty, deterioration during the turnover process, influx of persons with more limited means, and an overall decline in essential city services due to Detroit's declining tax base, have all played a part, as have the "spillover" effects of the deteriorating commercial structure. The continued spread of blight probably is the main overall problem in the Middle Zone, and the dominant concern of the numerous neighborhood citizen's councils that recently have formed.

One contributor to the spread of blight has come to be known as the "HUD House Fiasco." The foreclosure rate on FHA-insured mortgages in Detroit has been so great that the Department of Housing and Urban Development faces a management problem that is gargantuan in scope. Estimates from official sources of the number of HUD-owned homes in Detroit vary greatly; however, the figure probably is between fifteen and twenty thousand, or approximately 25 percent of all HUD-owned properties in the country. Most homes are either vacant or abandoned. The repair, upkeep, management, and marketing of these houses has been marked by bureaucratic inefficiency, individual corruption, and general scandal of outstanding dimensions. The physical result is that the Middle Zone is pockmarked with vacant houses, some broken down and vandalized, some falling into disrepair, some subject to rehabilitation, but all having a further blighting effect upon neighboring properties and streets.

Among the other problems of the Middle Zone is a school system that has declined in quality, that is in almost constant uncertainty concerning the adequacy of funds, and that has an increasingly bad public image. This image probably is one of the main reasons for the rapidity of suburban migration out of the zone. The school system also suffers from the rapid social upheavals that have taken place in the Middle Zone. There are some school districts where facilities are not fully utilized due to declining enrollments, many more where facilities are quite unable to handle the burgeoning influx of new pupils, some with virtually all black enrollments in racially mixed neighborhoods, and many which have become the scene for racial confrontation.

Lastly, of all the processes affecting the Middle Zone, probably the most publicized is the presence of violent crime. The Middle Zone contributes greatly to the city of Detroit's reputation as the nation's homicide capital. The high incidence of violent crime is related integrally to the tensions and frustrations created by social upheaval, but also is linked to Detroit's drug traffic and to an exceedingly high handgun ownership. Though probably not as great as the national image might imply, crime and the fear of crime have a strong influence on the life of the Middle Zone, as is visibly evident in the swelling number of protective devices and socially evident in the tendency to avoid going out in the evening hours.

In introducing the Middle Zone, it was suggested that what happens there might be the key to Detroit's future. That suggestion might well be extended to say that what happens in the Middle Zone is the key to the future of urban America. Looking at the Middle Zone in the summer of 1974, that future does not look promising. The forces described here— namely, the outward movement of long term residents, racial transition and its attendant instability, spread of blight, increase of crime, and a decline in the quality of schools and other social services—appear to be dominant. Furthermore, although the processes have been described as if they were independent entities, they comprise an interrelated whole of great complexity. That very complexity tends to point up the scarcity of know-how and means to counteract the processes. Federal, state, and city funds are tied to limited programs that hardly approach the real and complex causes of the problems.

Perhaps one source of optimism is the widespread recognition that the problems exist. Federal (the Department of Housing and Urban Development), state (the Michigan State Housing Development Authority) and city (the Community Development Commission) departments are deeply involved in analyzing the problems. More significantly, the Middle Zone virtually has come alive with a plethora of organizations whose main concern is to attempt to stabilize their community. Thus far these developments largely represent a recognition of the problems rather than a framework for the solution of the problems. For a large part of the Middle Zone, such recognition has come too late. For the remainder, the future remains in doubt.

In assessing that future, the positive elements described in this section cannot be ignored. They include a legacy of solid, attractive, tree-lined residential areas; the vitality of an energetic, confident black community; and the presence of traditional ethnic neighborhoods. If neighborhoods are to be stabilized, and if the Middle Zone is not to become the deteriorated

Inner Zone of the next decade, then the positive elements must be maintained and given support to check the destructive forces of change.

SUBURBAN AREA OF RADIAL DEVELOPMENT

The Suburban Area of Radial Development houses the dominant decisionmaking forces of the Detroit system. A blend of specific leadership activities and characteristic residence types has given this zone a role which in former times, and even today in certain parts of the world, was considered the prerogative of the central city. This blend also has created a lifestyle and outlook that contrasts markedly with those of other zones of the Detroit system.

The Radial Development Zone comprises a series of suburban sectors extending outward from the city of Detroit to the northeast, northwest, east, and south (Figure 2). By far the largest is to the northwest, encompassing much of southern Oakland County, and neatly dissecting the vast, semicircular area of suburban Detroit. Other sectors include a narrow finger of suburban growth along Lake St. Clair toward Mt. Clemens in the northeast, an interrupted corridor extending from West Dearborn to Ypsilanti and Ann Arbor in the west, and a small group of suburbs on the Detroit River to the south.

The spatial development of the zone within the Detroit system can be explained by a simple growth model. First, the nuclei of growth were early suburbs, such as Royal Oak, Birmingham, and Grosse Pointe, that grew along the series of radial arteries extending outward from the city of Detroit. These included a few elite residential suburbs attracted to physical amenities such as Lake St. Clair to the east, Grosse Isle on the Detroit River to the south, and the northeast-southwest belt of lake-filled morainic hills to the northwest. Second, these suburbs were consolidated, extended, and widened during the surge of suburban expansion following World War II that has continued to the present. In the Radial Zone the surge largely reflected the movement of higher income professional and white collar workers attracted by the prestige and amenities of well-established communities. Third, this movement in turn attracted high class shopping centers, professional and

business offices, research centers, and educational institutions. Fourth, continued growth was ensured by the construction of the Detroit area's main expressways. Finally, the zone developed gradually into what it is today —namely, a balanced pattern of upper and middle income residential areas; relatively adequate services and amenities to serve those areas; an excellent expressway network; and the majority of the important service, professional, and leadership activities of the Detroit metropolitan system. The zone has received virtually none of the postwar heavy industrial growth of that system.

During all these growth stages, the particular significance of this Oakland County sector has been reinforced. This sector is in the northwest, Detroit's traditional direction of expansion. It straddles Woodward Avenue, the spine of the Detroit system, as well as the important Grand River artery. The area between these two radial arteries is unique in the Detroit area because no railroad or industrial corridor has preempted and determined its land use and landscape. This has permitted the coalescence of the residential, business, and professional activities of the two arteries. The resulting sector is the largest and most characteristic sector of the Radial Zone.

The high socioeconomic status of the zone is suggested in most indexes of social and economic conditions. Residents of the zone are predominantly white, are wealthier, have more formal education, occupy more expensive and better quality homes, are more mobile, and are more likely to be in executive, professional, and service occupations than the residents in any other part of the Detroit system. If those indexes were mapped, statistics would tend to peak in certain communities, most significantly in Birmingham and Bloomfield Hills in the northwest sector, but also in the Grosse Pointes in the northeast sector, Grosse Isle in the downriver sector, and in West Dearborn and Ann Arbor Township in the western sector. A striking indication of the zone's socioeconomic character is the fact that Oakland County, encompassing the zone's important northwest sector, was the county with the nation's highest average household-effective buying income in 1974.

The overall high socioeconomic status does not mean that the Area of Radial Development is a zone of uniformity. Indeed, a visitor would be struck by the zone's diversity. The flat lake plain terrain of Dearborn or Grosse Pointe contrasts markedly with the rolling, hilly landscape of Bloomfield Hills and Franklin Village. Older deteriorating housing in certain parts of Ferndale and Hazel Park is a striking counterpart to newly built housing in Rochester and Bloomfield Hills. The decidedly urban suburbs of Royal Oak and Ferndale have a quite different character from semirural Avon and Oakland townships. The predominantly Jewish ethnic makeup of suburbs like Oak Park and Southfield differs from the largely Protestant-Catholic composition of the majority of other suburbs. Most noticeably, relatively calm residential communities like Bloomfield Hills, Grosse Pointe, and Grosse Isle stand in direct contrast to bustling, congested commercial centers like Southfield and Troy. In sum, no obvious, tangible uniformity distinguishes this from other zones of the Detroit system. Rather, the key to understanding the Radial Zone is to be found in a certain similarity and/or complementarity of interests, viewpoints, perceptions, and lifestyles.

One important contributor to this similarity is a distinctive group of occupational roles. More so than in any other zone, persons in the Suburban Area of Radial Development are engaged either in administrative, executive, professional, and other leadership occupations or in services catering to those leadership occupations. Moreover, although these pursuits might appear to be diverse, they find a point of identity in their common association with the automobile industry. This association is most direct in the case of those working in administrative and technical offices of General Motors, Ford, and Chrysler. The tie is almost as close in the case of executives and white collar workers in companies involved with industrial design, advertising, public relations, systems analysis, finance, and communications. Finally, the association is found in the case of those engaged in the professions and in a wide variety of other services. The nature of those many occupational pursuits, focusing upon and dependent upon the automobile industry, has led to a professional interaction, a general understanding, and an identity of interests that are distinctive attributes of the Radial Zone.

Another contributor to the zone's identity is a self-contained set of residential, service,

and recreational amenities that are at once distinctive and also enable the zone's residents to be relatively independent of the remainder of the metropolitan system. The zone is well served by shopping centers, from the larger, more urbane Northland, Oakland, and Ann Arbor malls, to the more specialized and sophisticated Grosse Pointe Village, Somerset Mall, and downtown Birmingham. The zone contains excellent public schools, as well as such distinguished private institutions as Cranbrook, Detroit Country Day, and University Liggett. The zone's college population is served by the University of Michigan in Ann Arbor, Michigan State University in East Lansing, and Eastern Michigan University in Ypsilanti, as well as the zone's own Oakland University. Health and professional services are superior to those in other zones of the metropolitan system. The zone is studded with cultural centers like Cranbrook, Meadowbrook, Greenfield Village, Ann Arbor's Rackham Auditorium, and the Grosse Pointe War Memorial. Finally, the zone has a wide variety of amenities—from yacht clubs and golf clubs to theaters and fine restaurants—that more than cater to the zone's recreational needs. Thus, residents seldom have to look elsewhere in the metropolitan system for the general amenities of life. The executive and his white collar employee might commute to other parts of the system five times per week, but they tend to return and spend their nonworking time within their own zone. Events of the Detroit Symphony, the Detroit Institute of Arts, and the Fisher Theater in Detroit might be well and faithfully attended, but preperformance cocktails and after theater snacks normally are consumed in places like West Dearborn, Grosse Pointe, and Bloomfield Hills. When interests and amenities are sought outside the Radial Zone, they are more often found well beyond the Detroit metropolitan area than elsewhere within the metropolitan area.

These amenities of the Radial Zone have helped to promote a general commonality of lifestyle. Many aspects of that lifestyle differ little in different parts of the zone. A similarity of attitudes, concerns, and outlooks are expressed in the zone's many local newspapers. Branches of certain clothing chains crop up in downtown Birmingham, on the "hill" in Grosse Pointe, in Ann Arbor, in Somerset Mall in Troy, but nowhere else in the Detroit region. Certain types of stores—such as ski shops, wine stores, and boutiques—are concentrated in this zone. High schools in Ann Arbor, Brimingham, and Grosse Pointe might be bitter academic and sports rivals, but this rivalry in itself reflects a similarity of interests.

One important aspect of the area's lifestyle is its extension into the recreational areas of northern Michigan. For decades, many residents have had summer homes in communities like Walloon Lake, Harbor Springs, and Mackinac Island. In more recent years, increasing mobility, more leisure time, and modern expressways have brought increasing numbers of the zone's residents to northern Michigan's lake resorts, ski areas, and recreational subdivisions. Although residents look upon this weekend and summer migration as an escape to a different environment, its ultimate effect has been to incorporate that environment into the lifestyle of the Radial Zone. In other words, northern recreation areas have become mere extensions of the zone's living patterns. Many of the zone's residents are more familiar with downtown Traverse City and Petoskey than with downtown Detroit.

The resident's relationships with other zones of the Detroit system are largely transactional. For many the vast area of metropolitan Detroit is perceived as a set of points connected by a series of lines. The points are the familiar places that are part of daily or periodic transactional activities—the G.M. Tech Center, the Fisher Building, Metropolitan Airport, the Detroit Athletic Club, WWJ radio, and the Ford Auditorium. The lines are the expressways, telecommunication lines, and air waves that interconnect those places and tie them to the Radial Zone. The metropolitan area underlying those points and lines tends to be unfamiliar territory. Increasingly it becomes unnecessary to go to other zones, to know what it is like there, or to understand their problems. To a significant degree, the Radial Zone resident is able to abstract himself from those problems and feel that they are outside his own spatial realm.

Emphasizing the self-contained nature of the Radial Zone in no way implies that the zone is static or unaffected by external events. Forces of change engulf this zone as they do other zones of the Detroit system. Many inner portions of the zone display symptoms of the blight that is so pronounced in other parts of the metropolitan area. Outer edges are being transformed rapidly by the actions of specu-lators and land developers. Traffic congestion plagues certain communities, often more than in other zones. Unprecedented recreational developments in northern Michigan have interrupted the exclusiveness of the zone's weekend living patterns. The threat of school busing influences residential decisions. Drugs, once considered a problem of the distant inner city ghetto, now appear as an integral part of the local high school scene. Residents realize that these external forces are affecting their life patterns, just as they are aware of the economic and social changes—such as federal pressure for improved auto emission standards, competition from foreign automobile imports, and a looming oil crisis—that impinge upon their occupational activities.

To a degree the Radial Zone resident is better able to adjust to these forces of change, and perhaps control them, than the resident of any other zone of the Detroit system. He has at his disposal both the information to know what are possible courses of action, and the financial and political power to take those actions. Traditionally those actions have been of two types. One is the "buffer" type—the use of decisionmaking powers such as political incorporation, pressure on Highway Commissions, and influencing of state legislators to screen out the forces of impending change. The other is the "relinquishment" type. Homeowners in Ferndale and Royal Oak buy homes in Troy and Clawson. An apartment dweller in Southfield moves to a condominium in Rochester. The Jewish Community Center leaves Oak Park to be reestablished in Bloomfield Township. Store owners relinquish their rental options in older shopping centers to rent space in currently fashionable malls. Even residents of prosperous Birmingham are prospective purchasers of property in Avon or Oakland Township. In sum, traditional reactions to forces of change have led to two significant spatial processes. One might be termed the "sifting" process, as certain elements move through the zone, generally in an outward direction. The other is the "shifting" process, as the zone itself extends outward to incorporate a wider area.

A striking yet characteristic aspect of those two spatial processes is the fact that they are so easily incorporated into the framework of the life patterns within the Radial Zone. When residents relinquish one community, they do not thereby give up the lifestyle of that community. Eventually they bring that lifestyle with them. As the locale shifts, the amenities associated with that locale also shift, often with little perceptible break in ongoing life patterns. At present, many residents are moving from Royal Oak, Ferndale and Oak Park as smoothly as they or their parents previously did from Detroit and Highland Park.

In the years to come the boundaries of the Suburban Area of Radial Development will continue to change, in keeping with the processes that have been described here. A more significant question is whether there will be changes in the characteristics utilized to describe the zone. In other words, will the zone's residents continue to control, or adjust to, impinging forces of change and maintain their distinctive lifestyles? To the degree that those forces are tangible, and within the framework of the present American societal structure, the answer would seem to be positive. More than his counterpart in any other zone, the Radial Zone resident has a controlling voice in that structure. It is highly unlikely that a zone that has been introduced by terms like "leadership" and "decisionmaking" would be unable to maintain its distinctive place within and outside of the Detroit system.

SUBURBAN AREA OF INTERSECTORAL DEVELOPMENT

The Suburban Area of Intersectoral Development contains much of the essential manufacturing work force of the Detroit system. A variety of highly skilled tradesmen, blue collar workers, and white collar office workers gives the zone an average income well above that of similar middle income zones in other U.S. metropolitan systems. This relative prosperity, as well as a general similarity in personal and family backgrounds, have contributed to a distinctive set of life patterns and a particular general outlook.

The spatial development of this Intersectoral Zone is connected intimately with the war time and postwar expansion of the automobile industry, an expansion that virtually transferred the industry from its fairly compact concentration in Detroit, Highland Park, Hamtramck, and Dearborn to a series of industrial corridors following the main railroads leading into the city. Those corridors were found in the broad

rural, interstitial areas between the sectors of Radial Development (Figure 2). The establishment of major automobile plants was followed by the swarming of ancillary metal and machinery industries, and the extension of residential subdivisions which caught up with the original factories and eventually engulfed them.

Today, those areas comprise a set of broad suburban wedges extending outward from the Detroit city limits and more or less alternating with the sectors of the Suburban Radial Area of Development. Two wedges dominate. The first is the broad wedge to the north, lying between the Woodward and Gratiot radials. Its postwar development was stimulated by industrial growth along the Mound Road Industrial Corridor and, to a lesser extent, along the Groesbeck Industrial Corridor. The filling in of this wedge explains Macomb County's position as the fastest growing county in the Detroit area during the past two census periods. The second is the equally broad wedge to the southwest, fanning from the Detroit River to encompass much of southern Wayne County, The development of this wedge reflects the auto-industry-dominated Central Wayne Corridor, the steel-chemical-oriented Downriver Corridor, and the "anchoring" effect of the Ford Motor Company complex in Dearborn. A third and narrower wedge stretches westward along the Plymouth Industrial Corridor in the northern part of Wayne County.

The nature of suburban growth within the Intersectoral Zone largely has determined its landscape. With the exception of sites preempted by industry, the zone was open to unfettered, low density sprawl. Generally no older suburbs existed to serve as nuclei for development. Often natural landscape features were obliterated to create monotonous subdivisions. Frequently services and amenities were not provided, so that the extensive shopping plazas serving the area often appear as peripheral afterthoughts rather than integrally planned units. One notable feature of the zone's development was the rapidity and variety of political incorporation. A common form was to take over whole townships, or what was left of whole townships. Thus suburbs like Warren, Sterling Heights, Westland, Taylor, and Southgate have at various periods become the fastest growing cities in the metropolitan area. Overall, however, the political development of the zone has left a haphazard array of incorporated

units, some developing into viable and co-
hesive suburbs, others plagued by poor services,
lack of structure, and often premature blight.

Today the visitor to almost any part of the
Intersectoral Zone has an image of neverending
suburban land. This land has a good deal of
variation. Neat, clean, but repetitious bungalow
subdivisions give way to new condominium
developments. Spacious school buildings surrounded by large playing fields in some suburbs
contrast with the smaller inadequate school
facilities in others. Gigantic new one story
automobile plants with spacious parking lots
and impressive landscaping, contrast with the
grubby congested streets of tool and die shops
that surround them. Large new shopping plazas
have a different visual effect than the uncoordi-
nated commercial strip developments on many
traffic arteries. Variety, however, does not
mean structure. The same visitor will look in
vain for "centers," "downtowns," and "main
streets" to give him a sense of organization and
orientation. He becomes aware that some political pattern exists only when he sees an
occasional sign telling him he is now entering
the "City of_____".

If this political pattern has little coincidence
with the suburbanite's daily activity pattern, it
has a profound influence upon his welfare.
Political boundaries in the Intersectoral Zone
have another meaning. Often they are the
means of preserving exclusiveness, of maintain-
ing separation, and of providing buffers against
outside encroachment. Most meaningful is a
suburb's exclusive claims to the tax base of
enterprises within its boundaries. Thus cities
like Warren, which houses the General Motors
Tech Center and other key automobile plants,
are able to maintain among the lowest taxes
and some of the finest municipal and school
services in the Detroit system. Almost as
meaningful is an incorporated unit's ability,
by legal or illegal means, to specify the nature
of its residents. Most suburbs have thus far
been able to exclude low income subsidized
federal housing developments, effectively chan-
neling virtually all such housing into only one
or two specific suburbs. In the same vein, many
suburbs have been able to exclude blacks, a
policy that has funneled black suburban migration into those few suburbs, such as Inkster, Ecorse, and River Rouge, that have a long
history of black settlement.

The socioeconomic characteristics of the
Intersectoral Zone might best be summarized
by looking at average family incomes. Although
residents are not as affluent as those in the
Suburban Area of Radial Development, they
are wealthier by far than persons in the Detroit
Inner and Middle zones and those in outlying
rural zones. Moreover, if comparisons were
made with similar middle income suburban
zones in other American metropolitan systems,
the intersectoral area would rank high. This is
explained by the zone's occupational structure.

The Intersectoral Zone houses one of the
largest technically skilled work forces in the
country. Contrary to popular misconception,
the typical member of that work force is not
the assembly line worker. Rather, he is the
specialist in one of the multitude of complex
technical and organizational tasks upon which
the American automobile industry depends.
Within automobile factories, those specialties
include titles like maintenance engineer, press
operator, foreman, shipping supervisor, die
caster, toolmaker, and quality inspector. Such
specialties are repeated in the thousands of
private companies—tool and die shops, engi-
neering shops, metal-cutting plants, heat treat-
ment plants—which depend upon the automobile
industry and, conversely, upon which the
automobile industry ultimately depends. The
manufacturing work force is supplemented by
workers in shipping companies, freight-handling
firms, fuel dealers, lumber specialists, and
other firms serving the main manufacturing
concerns. This array of specialized production
workers is complemented by an equally broad
and varied force of office personnel. In sum,
the zone provides much of the skilled and
experienced technical work force upon which
the Detroit, and indeed the American, automobile industry is based.

In many respects the zone's role within the
Detroit industrial system corresponds to that
played by the Detroit Middle Zone in previous
generations. In historical perspective, it is indeed a transplantation of the Middle Zone, as
younger families moved out to new subdivisions
in keeping with the war time and postwar
expansion of industrial activities. The direction-
al bias of this transplantation was decidedly
sectoral. Families from Detroit's east side and
from Hamtramck moved into the Macomb
County wedge; whereas those from Detroit's
west side, from East Dearborn, and from River
Rouge moved into the western and southwest-

ern wedges. This explains the ethnic makeup of parts of the Intersectoral Zone. Many young families who occupied the zone's new subdivisions were second and third generation offspring of Detroit's older immigrant ethnic communities. Thus parts of Roseville and East Detroit are a youthful extension of Detroit's Gratiot Avenue Italian Colony. The strongly Polish composition of Warren and Sterling Heights reflects families whose parents lived in Hamtramck. The Polish and Hungarian populations of Allen Park, Taylor, and Southgate stem from older concentrations of those nationalities in western and south-western Detroit and River Rouge. If the industrial role analogy is carried further, it might be suggested that the skills and know-how which operate the Chrysler truck assembly plant in Warren, the Ford stamping plant in Woodhaven, and the Great Lakes steel mill in Trenton are a product of experiences gained in the preceding generation in the Dodge Main plant in Hamtramck, the Kelsey-Hayes wheel factory on Livernois, and the iron foundries in Delray, respectively.

The characteristics discussed here—recency of development, sprawl of landscape, relative prosperity, common occupational interests, similar family backgrounds—have had an influence upon the general lifestyles within the zone. Those lifestyles have many facets. They tend to be family oriented, taking pride in homeownership and a personal interest in the local subdivision and the recently incorporated city or village. Activities are largely circumscribed by and dependent upon the personal automobile, as expressed visually by the vast, sprawling parking lots of shopping centers, schools, and commercial facilities. The outdoors is treasured, as typified by an abundance of sporting goods stores, or the hallowed nature of the annual deer season pilgrimage to the north. The zone likely accounts for a considerable proportion of the state sales of power boats, snowmobiles, and motor bikes. The recent boom in house trailer and camper ownership and the increasing desire to purchase lots in the booming northern recreational subdivision developments indicate that those outdoor interests continue unabated. However, those interests have not disassociated the resident from his city background and ethnic heritage, a fact that becomes apparent on a visit to one of the zone's taverns, bars, community halls, bowling alleys, or Friday night fish fries.

In sum, the lifestyle of the Intersectoral Zone incorporates the expansive, consumer-oriented outlook of American suburbia with certain traditional values learned in ethnic communities in the inner city. The blend is not complete, and the style still is being created.

Residents of the Intersectoral Zone have a distinctive set of relationships with, and attitudes toward, other zones in the Detroit system. There is considerable interaction with the Suburban Area of Radial Development, as the residents utilize the amenities of that zone such as shopping, professional services, and restaurants, and as residents of the two zones share certain citywide events such as baseball games, boat shows, conventions, and occasional civic functions. Those shared activities are not carried over into everyday interests and social life, which for the resident are closely identified with his own zone and with persons in that zone. Interaction with the Detroit Inner and Middle zones is of the functional nature described in the introduction to this section. For example, workers from Detroit man the assembly lines of Intersectoral Zone factories. Residents of the zone make visits to parents and grandparents in older city ethnic communities. Otherwise, the attitude of the Intersectoral Zone resident toward the two Detroit zones tends to be clear cut. He is conscious of the problems that exist in those zones, and one of his primary concerns is to keep those problems away from his own life.

In recent years many persons in the Intersectoral Zone have come to feel that their lifestyle is being undermined by a number of unforeseen social changes. Of particular concern is the question of an incorporated unit's control over its own affairs, an important reason for incorporation in the first place. For example, efforts to exclude nonwhites from local communities are increasingly hard to justify at a time when integration is being enforced in other parts of the country. Communities receiving various forms of federal aid find it hard to argue that they should not also provide space for low income public housing projects. Even such a sine quo non as local control over local schools paid for by local taxes is apparently being affected. In the years 1972 and 1973 many of those changes were clearly pointed up by the celebrated school busing issue.

These social forces represent problems from

which many residents believed they had es-
caped, and often are viewed as threatening a
way of life they have struggled hard to attain.
Moreover, values now being threatened are
values emphasized by a system that has paid
lip service to independence and local control.
The more dramatic responses to the forces of
social change are well publicized, such as the
overtly antiblack actions of certain suburban
mayors, the flood of "this family won't be
bused" signs on house doors and automobile
bumpers, as well as numerous confrontations
and demonstrations. The insecurity underlying
those responses is not always understood, nor
is the uncertainty concerning what those social
forces will mean in the future.

Even more recently, residents of the Intersectoral Zone have been confronted with a
more immediate threat to their accustomed
way of life, this time economic. Probably more-
so than in other similar suburban zones throughout the country they are affected directly by
the likelihood of a continued severe recession.
In the past, the relatively high incomes within
the zone have mirrored the overall prosperity
of the automobile industry. Characteristically,
that industry today was more severely affected
by the recession of the 1970s than almost any
other industry. The Intersectoral Zone, like
the Detroit system in general, was faced with a
higher than average rate of recession and
unemployment. When recessions are long and/
or severe, residents of the Intersectoral Zone
face an economic crisis that threatens a lifestyle that has been built up during almost three
decades. The insecurity brought about by that
threat compounds the more long term sense of
insecurity brought about by impinging social
forces.

It is the degree of this insecurity that dif-
ferentiates Intersectoral Zone residents from
those in the Suburban Area of Radial Development. For in spite of a relatively high economic
status, alternatives are limited. Inflation makes
it increasingly difficult to maintain an accustomed lifestyle. Recession in the auto
industry is a factor beyond their control. They
may change jobs, but they do not create jobs
or determine where those jobs are going to be.
They may move their place of residence, but
they are unsure whether their acquired lifestyle
will accompany them. Even if a new subdivision today appears isolated from present

forces of social change, there is no assurance
that it will remain isolated in the future.

In sum, much of the Suburban Area of Intersectoral Development is affected by processes of social and economic change that had not
been foreseen and that still are not fully understood. Although some responses have been
defensive and even violent, the majority of
residents is more passive, seeing few ways of
coping with those forces. The future of the
Suburban Area of Intersectoral Development
would seem to depend upon how those external
forces continue to unfold.

ZONE OF INTERCITY CORRIDOR GROWTH

The Zone of Intercity Corridor Growth expresses the basic urban pattern of southeastern
Michigan and is the framework for the ongoing
urbanization processes taking place in that
region. A close interdependence between the
zone's cities and the Detroit metropolis make it
an integral part of the Detroit system.

The zone comprises a series of six urban corridors radiating out from Detroit and connecting Detroit with all important cities in its
hinterland (Figure 2). In clockwise sequence
those corridors are known as the Detroit-Toledo Corridor, the Detroit-Jackson Corridor, the
Detroit-Lansing Corridor, the Detroit-Bay City
Corridor, the Detroit-Port Huron Corridor, and
the Detroit-London (Ontario) Corridor. The
Detroit-Bay City Corridor is in the most advanced stages of urbanization, with the Detroit-
London Corridor the least advanced.

The development of the corridors has been
an important theme in Michigan history. They
were the routes of early Indian trails that
focused upon Cadillac's Fort Pontchartrain on
the Detroit River. They became the sites of
military roads during the period of American
settlement, and thus the means of settlement
of the interior. They dictated the locations of
early towns in the area. They have remained the
dominant arteries of southern Michigan right
up to the present, eventually becoming the
framework of the present day expressway system. Today they are the basis of the corridor
growth that is the dominant feature of urban
land use development.

Similarity in overall historical development
does not mean that the zone's various corri-

dors are alike. Each corridor is distinctive. Most significantly, each differs in its degree of urban development, in the functional structure of its cities, and in the nature of its interdependence with metropolitan Detroit.

The dominant corridor by far is the Detroit-Bay City Corridor, interconnecting the cities of Detroit, Pontiac, Flint, Saginaw, and Bay City. The corridor points northwest, the traditional magnet for the Detroit system's growth. Its importance has been reinforced by the functional economic interdependence of its main cities. Largely this reflects the presence of the General Motors Corporation, whose main enterprises are located there (for example, the Pontiac Division in Pontiac, the Chevrolet and Buick divisions in Flint, and the Steering Gear Division in Saginaw). The company not only dominates economic activities but has left its stamp upon the character, appearance, identity, and lifestyles of the cities in the corridor. The corridor continues to be the dominant focus of urban expansion in southeastern Michigan; urban development is virtually complete between Detroit and Bay City.

Second in importance is the Detroit-Jackson Corridor, connecting Detroit, Ypsilanti, Ann Arbor, and Jackson, and extending farther to Battle Creek and Kalamazoo. The corridor is "anchored" by the Ford Motor Company's Dearborn complex, and automobile-related activities are found in other cities. However, the corridor's character is set by other factors. Most important is the presence of several of Michigan's main educational institutions, including Eastern Michigan University in Ypsilanti, The University of Michigan in Ann Arbor, and Western Michigan University in Kalamazoo, as well as distinguished private colleges like Albion College in Albion and Kalamazoo College in Kalamazoo. Those institutions strongly influence the nature and lifestyle of cities in the corridor and promote a high degree of interdependence between those cities and the educational and research institutions of the city of Detroit. Interaction within the Detroit-Jackson Corridor is further enhanced by the presence of the Detroit system's metropolitan airport. Today the chain of urbanization is largely uninterruped between Detroit and Ann Arbor.

The Detroit-Toledo Corridor ranks third in importance. This connects Detroit with an important industrial and commercial center, parallels a strategic link of the Great Lakes waterway, and forms Detroit's main outlet to the population centers, markets, and general economic life of mid-America. However, urban growth in this corridor is not as great as these considerations might warrant. This apparent anomaly would seem to reflect two factors. First, the corridor points away from the northwest, the traditional growth axis of the Detroit system. Second, the intense functional interdependence between its cities, so pronounced in other corridors, is lacking. Thus, despite its important transportational role, the Detroit-Toledo Corridor is less an integral part of the Detroit system, and less a representative segment of that system's society than the corridors to the northwest and west.

The Detroit-Lansing Corridor connects metropolitan Detroit with Brighton, Lansing, and eventually with Grand Rapids. The corridor has not been a dominant focus of urbanization like the two corridors which border it. The main city, Lansing, is relatively distant from Detroit, and intervening towns have not become growth centers. However, this situation is changing rapidly as Detroit sprawls along the Grand River artery; as industrial, educational, and recreational functions spill over from the two adjacent growth arteries; and as distances are reduced by the I-696 expressway. These developments enhance the importance of the one function that sets the character of the corridor —namely, state government. Indeed, this corridor expresses the increasing interdependence between state and metropolis, connecting Lansing—the state capital; Grand Rapids— the state's major nonmetropolitan city; and East Lansing—site of the state's largest undergraduate university; with the Detroit region.

The Detroit-Port Huron Corridor is less developed. It leads to the northeast, away from the Detroit system's major growth axes, and toward Port Huron, one of the zone's smaller urban centers. The recent surge of urban expansion, which already has engulfed the city of Mt. Clemens, will likely continue. However, this reflects more the independent growth of metropolitan Detroit than the functional interdependence among cities of the corridor.

The last corridor connects Detroit with Windsor, Chatham, London, and beyond. The corridor plays a dominant transportational role, connecting the Detroit-Windsor metropolis with southern Ontario and with the eastern United States through the Niagara peninsula. Urban growth has taken place in all of the corridor's cities, but urban coalescence is not as marked as in other corridors. As the "spine" of southwestern Ontario, the Detroit-London Corridor will see increased urban growth in the future. The character of the resulting urban corridor will be less strongly influenced by its interconnections with the Detroit metropolis.

It is likely that intercity corridor growth will continue to set the pattern of ongoing urbanization in Southern Michigan. The processes involved will be expansion of individual cities in the corridors; coalescence, as corridor cities gravitate towards each other; extension of certain corridors; and widening, as corridors encroach over adjacent land. Moreover, incipient urban corridors promise to connect the radial corridors in a circumferential belt—Port Huron-Flint-Lansing-Jackson-Toledo —to create a weblike pattern. As in the past, dominant growth corridors will be those to the northwest and west.

As urbanization progresses, the specialized functional interdependence between cities in individual corridors will intensify, and the resultant character and lifestyle of individual corridors will become increasingly distinctive. It would appear that the essential sectoral patterning of social life in the Detroit system will continue as the system continues to expand.

ZONE OF RURAL CHANGE

The Zone of Rural Change is the part of the Detroit system that is not developed in the sense implied by present-day planners, but its landscape characteristics and activities are determined largely by forces emanating from that system. The zone is more extensive than any other zone, located in between the intercity growth corridors but beyond the contiguous built-up part of metropolitan Detroit (Figure 2). The zone incorporates the northern parts of Oakland and Macomb counties and a smaller portion of western Wayne County in the SMSA as well as a considerable part of

adjacent Monroe, Washtenaw, and St. Clair counties.

There are two physiographic sections. One is the relatively flat glacial lake plain—the Erie-St. Clair Lowland—bordering the northeast-southwest trending waterway between Lakes Huron and Erie and extending roughly twenty-five miles inland from the waterway. This plain traditionally has supported a prosperous mixed agricultural economy of dairying, meat animals, cash crops, and horticultural products. The second part is the hilly, uneven lake-pitted interlobate moraine—the Thumb Upland—bordering the lowland belt to the northwest. This area has been more conducive to recreational developments, although limited patches of dairy farming and fruit growing have been important.

Today those traditional rural activities have become secondary. The main characteristics of different parts of the zone are important in terms of their relationship to ongoing forces of urbanization. These forces include urban sprawl and urban shadow. The first refers to the active land conversion processes taking place at the area's built-up edges. Urban shadow refers to the long stagnation process which appears to condemn a rural area to declining productivity and general sterility. Together they explain the landscape variation in the zone.

One aspect of that landscape variation is the evidence of what appears to be traditional agricultural types, such as dairy farming or field cropping. This evidence generally is illusionary. Closer examination shows that agriculture has declined, both in quality and in intensity. Often operators are too old to manage the farm efficiently, and their children show little interest in farming. More often operating costs—like increased land values, higher taxes, and competition for farm labor— have forced farmers to look for new farms farther away from the urbanization process. Where built-up areas are close, farming is impeded by noise, trespassing, trash, and drainage disruption. All of these factors lead the farmer to invest less time, labor, and capital, particularly in activities that provide a long term financial return.

The second landscape feature is idle land, with vast stretches of neglected grass, weeds, brush, trash, and derelict farm buildings, owned either by speculators or by farmers intending to sell the land at the most profitable time. Because farm abandonment appears to increase at a much faster rate than physical urbanization, the area of derelict land continues to expand. "Idleness" is the most widespread land use in the Zone of Rural Change.

The overall landscape variation is punctuated by spots of more intense activities where landowners temporarily have capitalized upon the recreational needs of nearby suburban residents. For example, horse farms and riding stables are common in many sections, to the degree that Oakland and Washtenaw counties have the highest "horse" densities in Michigan. Elsewhere, cider mills have seen a rejuvenation, offering a range of activities that transcends the simple sale of cider. Trapshooting, golf courses, and other recreational activities are additional amenities offered.

Last, the general appearance of idleness and inactivity in most of the Zone of Rural Change contrasts strikingly with the "sprawl" at the zone's urbanized edges. Here the different actors in the land conversion process—speculator, developer, builder, realtor, utility worker, homeowner, politician, and planner—indulge in the rapid succession of negotiations and decisions ending in development. In such areas the landscape shows the full brunt of change, as land is cleared, utility ditches are dug, streets partitioned, bulldozers utilized, dust created, and the shells of future buildings erected.

The resulting landscape pattern in the Zone of Rural Change is not haphazard. In areas such as the broad intersectoral wedges to the north and southwest, where there has been a relatively even spread of suburban land use into flat and productive agricultural land, there is a distinct sequence of the landscape types described above. Elsewhere the order is not so discernible. The confusing pattern of preexisting land use and the spotty nature of the urban sprawl process have patterned the landscape into something more akin to a mosaic.

Today the zone provides the locale where new processes of change are operating and where new tensions are being created. Many of these processes are physical, associated with urbanization forces which have been discussed. A new subdivision is built at the urban edge. An expressway is extended into a different area. A new automobile plant is built in a nonindustrial village. A sewer line is con-

structed. Other processes are less obvious. There is a general "sifting" of landowners through the area, largely involving farmers who are forced to give up their farms because of encroaching urbanization but who are not ready to give up farming as a way of life. They sell the original farm and buy another farther away where taxes are lower and urban nuisances are fewer. There is also the steady movement into the zone of suburban residents whose economic activities are tied to the built-up metropolitan area but who wish to escape that area's problems. This escape can involve several jumps in a relatively short time.

Many of the processes operating in the Zone of Rural Change involve movements and migrations, predominantly in an outward direction. The farmer in western Wayne County buys a new farm in Monroe County. The Warren suburbanite who fears school busing of his children buys in a new subdivision in Washington Township. Realtors and developers who have developed the city of Troy, and are developing Avon Township, are now moving their activities to Oakland Township. Ford Motor Company, which first set up a factory in Warren, and later constructed another in the "rural" village of Utica, now builds another in "outlying" Romeo. The sectoral movements so characteristic of other Detroit zones are continued into the Zone of Rural Change.

These processes have produced tensions among the zone's residents. Ironically, the most important source of tension involves conflicting attitudes toward the very factor that created the zone in the first place, namely anticipated growth. Increasing numbers of residents, original landholders and newcomers alike, see growth as a threat to the landscape and lifestyle that attracted them to the area. This tension often leads to resistance. For example, a sewer line which is requisite to rational and planned development in northeast Macomb County is successfully opposed by local residents. Amenities like paved streets bring objections in parts of Oakland Township because they appear to be synonomous with development. A proposed billion dollar shopping center in Bloomfield Township is defeated by residents because it will promote growth and spoil the character of the area. Often the alignments in such confrontations appear to be incompatible. Older farmers side with developers to promote schemes that are opposed by residents who only recently arrived in the area. Plans of local planning commissions are resisted because their very rationality promotes the growth which the residents do not want.

In sum, the Zone of Rural Change has passed out of a previous rural recreational state and is destined for some sort of urban future. When and how that future will be attained is uncertain. Into the foreseeable future, the major part of the zone will remain in its present state of limbo, with a landscape characterized more by waste and idleness than by productive use. Meanwhile local processes are to be observed which are offshoots of the dominant force—urbanization—that has created the zone. The presence of this force emphasizes the integral place of the Zone of Rural Change within the Detroit system.

SUMMARY

In summary, the spatial model portrayed in Figure 2, though highly generalized, provides a convenient and meaningful framework for grouping Detroit society and discussing the different parts of the Detroit system. The zones in the model encompass areas and people with different backgrounds, lifestyles, outlooks, and concerns, and are subjected to quite different external processes. At the time of writing it would appear that the differences between the zones are becoming greater, and their respective societies more divergent. At the same time this increasing social differentiation between the zones does not diminish the essential functional interdependence among them. All continue to be integral parts of the Detroit system.

Forces of Change in the Detroit System

One theme which pervades any discussion of the Detroit system and its regions is change. Indeed, the very essence of the zones discussed above is the forces of change that are engulfing, and to a degree, transforming them. In the remainder of the study those forces are considered more systematically and in greater detail. The consideration is limited to three of the most important forces affecting the Detroit system. These are (1) renewal, which affects all parts of the Detroit system but is most pronounced in the Detroit Inner Zone; (2) racial change, which is most characteristic of the Detroit Middle Zone; and (3) expansion, which emanates from the Suburban Zones and impinges upon the Zone of Rural Change. The final section of this study examines the operation of these three processes in local situations. The present section acts as a bridge to the final section, looking at the three forces of change in the perspective of the total Detroit system.

RENEWAL

Renewal entails the deliberate clearance of existing facilities with the purpose of rebuilding and redeveloping an area into some different and theoretically improved use. Examples include urban renewal, highway construction, school construction, and institutional expansion. Renewal has had a considerable impact upon the Detroit system. This impact reflects a number of factors. First, renewal projects tend to be concentrated in specific areas,

where their visual impact tends to be overwhelming. Second, renewal projects have a distinct "rub-off" effect upon adjacent areas. Third, the renewal process affects individuals and families, who must be relocated. Fourth, the renewal process is slow. Years, even decades, pass between the time of announcement and eventual construction. The total effect is that renewal has a detrimental effect upon the appearance, image, and life of the city. Such has been the case for almost two decades in the Detroit inner city, where on the one hand an everexpanding expressway system has virtually chopped up the landscape, and on the other hand an urban renewal system has left many of the remaining parcels in varying states of decay, idleness, and reconstruction. This discussion of renewal begins with federally assisted urban renewal.

Urban Renewal

Although urban renewal includes other elements like neighborhood conservation and code enforcement, the most meaningful and dramatic form is that of complete redevelopment. Within the Detroit area redevelopment is concentrated largely in the Detroit-Highland Park-Hamtramck nucleus, in Pontiac, and in adjacent older suburbs such as East Dearborn, Royal Oak, Ferndale, and Centerline. However, this analysis concentrates on the city of Detroit, where the effects of redevelopment programs have been felt the most.

In aggregate Detroit's urban renewal program encompasses 1,505 acres, which at one

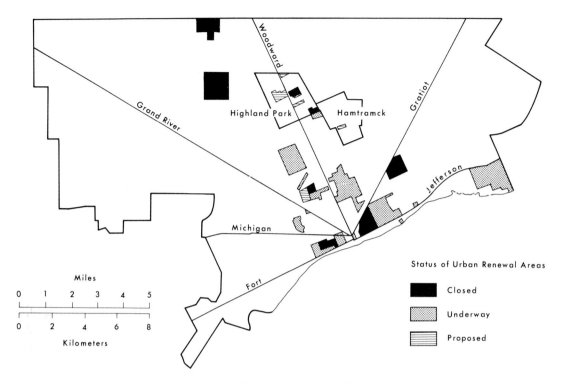

Figure 4. Urban renewal areas in Detroit, Highland Park, and Hamtramck.

time contained 17,133 housing units and 1,982 businesses. An estimated 7,660 families and 6,730 individuals had to be relocated. With some exceptions, the renewal projects are found within Grand Boulevard, particularly east and west of the central business district and adjacent to the Lodge and Chrysler expressways immediately to the north (Figure 4). Virtually all these areas were residential. They comprised the worst of Detroit's housing stock, although in some areas, such as the University City area, good quality dwellings were included. They also comprised some of the most vital and colorful of Detroit's ethnic and working class communities: "Black Bottom," "Paradise Valley," "Corktown," "Chinatown," and "Bagley" are an important part of Detroit's heritage.

These areas have been and are being renewed for a number of uses, many of which are not residential. Eight renewal projects, comprising 251 acres, are industrial. Three projects, comprising 160 acres, are institutional, notably in The University City and Medical Center area. Five listed projects are commercial, mainly in the central business district. Of the residential projects, a large proportion are for upper and middle income persons, particularly in the Gratiot, Lafayette, and Elmwood Park areas. Thus far, only a small percentage of the completed renewal areas has been made available for low income housing.

In the summer of 1974 three large parcels comprising 270 acres, and several smaller parcels, lay vacant with no projected use in the near future. The present vacant status of those parcels has been, at one time or another, the status of all renewal lands in Detroit. In effect, vacant land has been a pervasive and accepted part of the Detroit inner city landscape for more than two decades. This land has taken on various hues and physical characteristics, from bare earth and weeds, to green rural-like tranquility, to western sagebrush, and to a recent Detroit specialty, white wooden fences, which give vacant blocks in the heart of the city the appearance of Kentucky horse farms.

As in most American cities, the urban renewal process in Detroit has been long, complicated, and bureaucratic. In any single area the process might be divided into four phases: first, a consideration phase, in which the project is proposed, considered, rumored, announced, and eventually funded; second, a clearing phase, in which property is condemned, residents evicted and relocated, and property demolished; third, a vacant phase, in which land lies idle awaiting purchase and development; and finally, the development phase. Each of these phases has taken its toll in terms of human suffering and landscape deterioration. A detrimental aspect of the renewal process has been the long and uncertain time lag involved during and between each phase. Although some projects have taken at least ten years before the cycle is complete, some have taken twenty years, and some have not yet been completed. The time lag also incorporates changes in national temperament, including some basic changes in the philosophy of urban renewal itself.

One recent change in philosophy might well have an important influence on the future of urban renewal in Detroit. Although the change has been gradual, it clearly divides renewal policies and attitudes into two periods. The first period prevailed throughout much of the program, and was characterized by little real attempt to understand the plight of residents. Projects were discussed and planned with little local participation. Residents felt themselves to be at the mercy of a frightening combination of federal officials, city government, and the institutions that would benefit from development. Redevelopment often took place for private or institutional benefits, or for bureaucratic or financial expediency. The second period, inaugurated in the last few years, is a period of local and resident control, which has been brought about by a complex of factors including federal revenue-sharing stipulations, model neighborhood examples, the growing power of citizens councils, and probably a changing attitude on the part of city officials as to what constitutes "development."

The second period of Detroit's renewal history also has brought forth problems. Many local resident organizations understandably tend to be suspicious of any large scale development projects. As a result, large, worthwhile projects often are rejected or stymied, and actual development, though democratic, has the potential of being piecemeal, unplanned, and destined to bring about early community blight.

Thus, the future quality of urban renewal is open to question in Detroit. But the presence of urban renewal is there. Whatever the nature of eventual development, the process leaves large parts of the city with empty buildings, vacant land, and developments in varying degrees of completion.

Freeway Construction

A second kind of renewal is freeway construction. The Detroit system is well served by one of the most extensive freeway networks in the country. The construction of this network has occurred largely since the passage of the Federal Highway Act of 1956, when the Interstate system was initiated. In the Detroit SMSA alone there were in 1974 almost 200 miles of completed expressways, with approximately sixty-five miles under construction or scheduled for construction. Vast tracts of land formerly used for residential or commercial purposes are now part of the system. Even in the period before 1970 an estimated 20,400 homes in the Detroit metropolitan area had been demolished for expressway construction.

Most completed freeways follow the radial pattern that has been such a dominant feature of the Detroit area's development (Figure 5). The focus is on the central city, as most of the early freeways were designed to bring suburban residents to downtown workplaces. The Ford Freeway, about three miles north of the central business district, is aligned with the river-oriented street pattern of central Detroit, but outside the city it also assumes a radial form. Freeways presently under construction or proposed are designed to improve east-west or north-south connections in outlying or suburban areas. I-275 will traverse most of the north-south length of Wayne County, bypassing Metropolitan Airport and joining I-75 in Monroe County. I-96 will extend directly westward from the Jeffreys Freeway in central Detroit to serve a large western suburban area before being joined by I-275 at Plymouth. Most significantly, the I-696 Freeway paralleling Ten and Eleven Mile Roads is designed to fill the much-needed link among Detroit's northern suburbs. At present, stretches of those routes form broad swaths of bulldozed land sweeping through the suburban landscape. Other stretches are portrayed by rows of standing but vacant buildings from which former residents have been evicted and relocated. These kinds of landscapes have characterized,

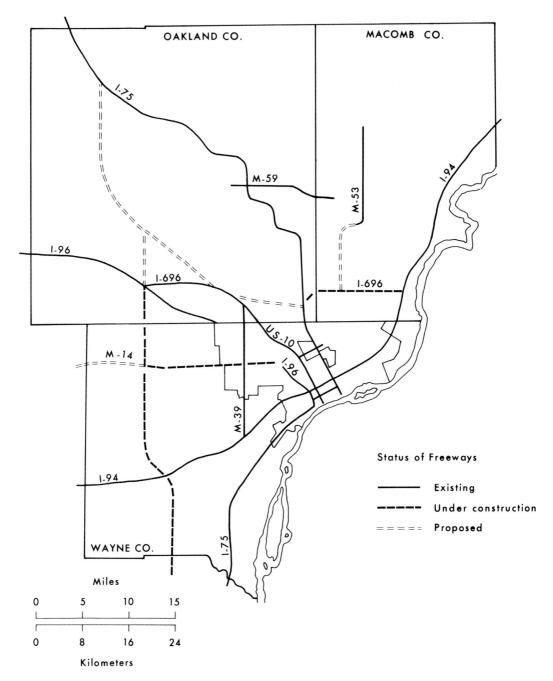

Figure 5. Detroit area freeways, 1974.

at one time or another, all areas where the present expressway system exists. Indeed, they have been an important part of the Detroit metropolitan scene for almost two decades.

Like other forms of renewal, the freeway construction process is lengthy and bureaucratic, with a series of long drawn out phases between initial announcement and final construction. During those phases the personal grief and landscape destruction characteristic of most renewal processes are compounded by the division of neighborhoods, shifting of travel patterns, cutting off of market areas, and increased travel time and congestion. The impact of the process has varied throughout the Detroit area, but it is the Inner Zone that is affected most, because most freeways converge upon the downtown area. In addition to all other adverse effects, many inner city communities have been split up or isolated. For example, the Hubbard-Richard community, a predominantly Mexican-American community west of the central business district, is today practically inaccessible. In suburban areas, lower income areas generally have been affected more than upper income areas. Partly this reflects the attraction in the former of lower property values which reduce right of way costs. Partly, it means that the wealthier have been more articulate, influential, and politically able to divert expressways from personal residential and business areas. In some cases, it means that expressway location has been used by planners as a slum clearance device.

The Detroit area has benefited greatly from the mobility provided by an excellent freeway network. At the same time, the area has paid its price. For almost two decades, the freeway construction process has brought instability and destruction to a considerable part of the metropolitan area.

Institutional Expansion

A third kind of renewal involves the location or expansion of public and private institutions into adjacent residential areas. This includes large scale institutions—such as Wayne State University or the Medical Center—highly visible on the city's landscape. It also includes schools and smaller scale projects that are less apparent but have a great cumulative impact on an area. Often the latter are associated with the changing needs and problems of the city, and include health clinics, drug abuse centers, nursing homes, the Salvation Army, and other religious missions.

The impact of institutional expansion upon the landscape and its residents is like that of other forms of renewal. However, additional factors are often involved. Because land is not always publicly acquired, property speculation can be great where expansion is anticipated. This can mean that residents are faced with unexpected rent increases that they cannot

afford. Moreover, an organized relocation program generally is absent, so that adjustment problems for displacees can be greater than those in federal renewal projects. Finally, many institutions are of the type that are felt to attract "undesirables." A Salvation Army soup kitchen can have an upsetting influence on neighborhood stability, particularly where children are present.

Although impossible to quantify, large tracts of land and large numbers of people are affected by institutional expansion. Examples are present throughout the Detroit area, but the process is most pronounced in the Inner Zone of Detroit. It is in this zone that the greatest number of large expanding institutions are to be found. Moreover, it is here that social agencies and institutions, often excluded from other areas, tend to congregate. Many parts of the Detroit Inner Zone face the prospect of being institutionalized out of existence by those very institutions whose presence is intended to bring about their betterment.

RACIAL CHANGE

The racial change process refers to the change of a residential neighborhood from all white to all black. This process has been rapid in Detroit. Over the past two decades from 7,000 to 9,000 Detroit households changed from white to black each year. Integrated neighborhoods are few. Normally whites accept a few black families in their neighborhoods, but when a critical proportion is reached, a massive exodus of white homeowners follows.

Between 1910 and 1930 Detroit's black population grew rapidly, from 5,700 to 120,000. Even with this increase blacks were a distinct minority in 1930, with 7.6 percent of the city's population. The large scale migration that transformed Detroit into one of the nation's leading black cities is a phenomenon associated with the "boom" years of World War II and the postwar period. Over the past three decades Detroit's black population more than quadrupled, whereas the white population decreased by 56 percent (Table 1). Most incoming blacks have come to the city of Detroit. Of the 757,000 blacks in the Detroit SMSA (18 percent of the SMSA's population), 660,000 are residents of the city of Detroit, and 23,000 of the remainder live in Detroit's enclaves, Hamtramck and

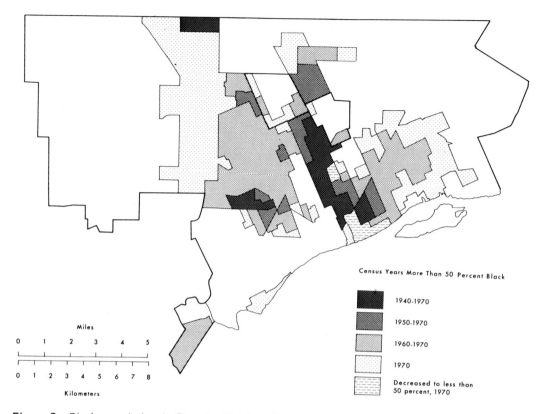

Census Years More Than 50 Percent Black

1940-1970

1950-1970

1960-1970

1970

Decreased to less than
50 percent, 1970

Miles

0   1   2   3   4   5

0   1   2   3   4   5   6   7   8

Kilometers

Figure 6. Black population in Detroit, Highland Park, and Hamtramck, 1940-1970. In the oldest ghetto areas the percentage black is decreasing. Source: U.S. Bureau of the Census.

Highland Park. The relatively small number of suburban blacks live in segregated sections of Pontiac and Mt. Clemens or in a limited number of older suburbs such as Inkster, Ecorse, and River Rouge. Most of suburban Detroit is typified by its three largest suburbs—Warren,

Table 1.   City of Detroit's Black Population 1910-1970

	Total Population (1000s)	Percent Black	Percent White
1910	466	1.2	98.8
1920	994	4.1	95.9
1930	1569	7.6	92.4
1940	1623	9.2	90.7
1950	1850	16.2	83.6
1960	1670	28.9	70.8
1970	1511	43.7	55.5

Source: U.S. Census of Population

Livonia, and Dearborn—which together in 1970 had a black population of 186 out of a total population of 393,568.

The spatial growth of Detroit's black community can be traced from a near east side nucleus at the turn of the century to the vast, sprawling, but still highly segregated community that it is today (Figure 6). Like many other Detroit immigrants, blacks first settled on the near east side, and by 1910 most of the black community lived in an area south of Gratiot with St. Antoine as its major business thoroughfare. Between 1910 and 1940 extension occurred into adjacent areas to the north and to the east. A narrow corridor extended north past East Grand Boulevard along John R., Brush, Beaubien, St. Antoine, and Hastings streets. The eastern extension was confined to "Black Bottom," an area bounded by Mt. Elliot to the east, Gratiot to the north, and Jefferson to the south. A third area of settlement was a narrow strip on the west side near Lawton between Warren and Tireman.

The doubling of Detroit's black population between 1940 and 1950 brought only a limited spatial expansion of the community, largely an extension of the north-south corridor into Highland Park. At that time a war time and postwar housing shortage prevailed. Families moved in with each other and housing units often were subdivided to accommodate the needs of the growing black population. In the 1940s black Detroit still was a spatially confined "ghetto" in the narrowest sense of the word.

This situation changed dramatically in the 1950s. The suburban building boom literally brought about a spatial "release" of the metropolitan area, which had its repercussions on Detroit's black community. Between 1950 and 1960 no fewer than eighty-three additional census tracts became 50 percent black compared to twenty-four in the previous decade. This involved the extension of all black settlement areas. The most notable trend was the movement into northwest Detroit, in a sector between James Couzens and Grand River (Figure 6).

This dominant northwesterly expansion continued into the 1960s, so that by 1974 the zone of greatest racial transition was located between Greenfield and the Southfield Expressway. On the east side this transition zone is located close to Chalmers Avenue. It is within these areas that the conditions and processes associated with racial change are to be found today. Similar conditions and processes have characterized, at one time or another, all areas of Detroit where racial change has taken place. As has been seen, they have been an essential aspect of the Detroit Middle Zone for more than two decades.

The process of racial change is highly complex. It begins long before transition takes place, as the awareness of impending change creates instability in white neighborhoods. It continues during the period of active transition, when the rapid sequence of events can bring turmoil, neighborhood deterioration, and personal conflicts. It is associated with a myriad of social problems, ranging from confrontation in schools to disruption of city services. It remains long after transition has taken place, because the instability and turmoil of previous periods often leave a legacy of neighborhood depreciation and blight. In recent years efforts have been made by local community groups to combat the more adverse effects of the transition process. The very existence of those groups is a recognition of the need for neighborhood stabilization and, in most cases, the realization that this stabilization requires a high degree of racial integration. In certain neighborhoods, their efforts have had considerable success. Whether that success is permanent or only temporary is still open to question, and perhaps is the key to the future of the outer parts of the city of Detroit. In areas closer to the city center, the more adverse effects of more than two decades of racial change have left their mark upon the city's landscape.

URBAN EXPANSION

Urban expansion entails the conversion of rural land to urban uses. In a sense the whole Detroit system has undergone expansion at one time or another. Normally, however, the term refers to the rapid suburbanization that has taken place during and since World War II. As has been seen, this suburbanization has led to the creation or expansion of the Suburban Area of Radial Development, the Suburban Area of Intersectoral Development, and the Zone of Intercity Corridor Growth. The rapidity of expansion is indicated in Figure 7, which shows the spread of the Detroit system's built-up area since 1940, and its status in 1970. Though varying in intensity from year to year, the expansion process goes on continually, as is seen in Table 2, which lists the amount of new residential construction in the southeast Michigan region since 1970.

Maps showing the expansion of the built-up area in no way indicate the scope and extent of the urban expansion process. For the process leaves its impact well beyond the edge of the built-up area, as rural areas undergo a slow transition period long before actual urbanization takes place. Although development

Table 2. Authorized New Dwelling Units in SEMCOG Region, 1970–1974

1970	1971	1972	1973	1974 (first six months only)
28,486	43,865	39,836	35,762	12,472

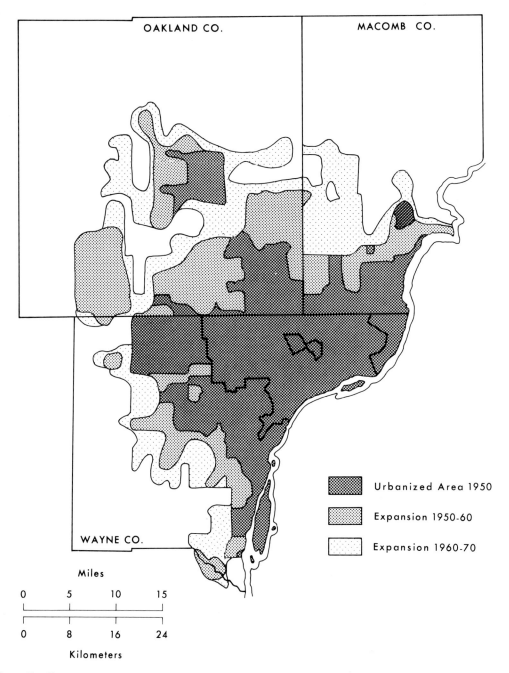

Figure 7. Expansion of the Detroit urbanized area, 1950–1970.

sometimes can take place rapidly, there is normally a period of years, and often decades, between the beginning of agricultural decline and the final urban development. This time lag can be measured in other terms, such as economic recessions and booms, changes in

mortgage rates, changes in zoning ordinances, gasoline crises, and a complex of other factors that not only influence the rate of development, but also whether development will ever take place.

Whatever the factors affecting the nature of

urban expansion, the physical presence of the process is visible throughout the Detroit system. The entire Zone of Rural Change is in one way or another affected by urban expansion processes, and this comprises a major part of southeastern Michigan. As has been the case for almost three decades, the largest area in the Detroit system lies in a state of transition, neither rural nor urban.

SUMMARY

In summary, a large part of the Detroit system today is subject to the impact of one or more of the forces of spatial change that have been described in this chapter. Moreover, an even larger part of the system has been subjected to those forces in the past few decades, and in some places the impact is still visible on the present-day landscape. The total influence of spatial change forces on the Detroit system is summarized by Sinclair in the following quotation from *The Face of Detroit:*

Unfortunately these forces tend to bring with them conditions of instability and uncertainty, which in turn lead to deterioration in areas undergoing change. In outlying parts of the Detroit area, urban sprawl has created large stretches of blighted vacant land, and often has led to unsound and poorly planned developments. Within the city, ghetto expansion has released forces of deterioration well in advance of the "front" of change. Processes associated with highway construction and urban renewal have left a considerable part of the central cities in a state of degenerating limbo. In total, conditions associated with spatial change are responsible for many of the Detroit area's strains.

This section has looked at the forces of change within the broad perspective of the total Detroit system. To describe more intimately how those forces operate, the scale of inquiry now is narrowed to a local level.

Forces of Change at the Local Level: Three Case Studies

The forces of change that are transforming such large parts of the Detroit system also have an impact at the local level. Indeed, all three of the forces described in the previous section have an influence in a wide variety of local situations. This section examines the operation of those forces in a number of selected areas in metropolitan Detroit. Three case studies have been selected. Each stands by itself as an individual entity. At the same time, each can be associated with one of the forces of change discussed in the last section, and identified with one or more of the major zones of the Detroit system analyzed previously. Thus, the Cass Corridor study examines the different forms of renewal taking place in the Detroit Inner Zone. The Northwest Detroit study focuses upon the racial change process, which is such a dominant feature of the Detroit Middle Zone. Finally, the Oakland Township study examines urban expansion at the interface between the Suburban Area of Radial Development and the Zone of Rural Change.

RENEWAL IN THE CASS CORRIDOR

The Cass Corridor is a one-and-a-half square mile inner city neighborhood located between downtown Detroit and Wayne State University, bounded on the east by Woodward Avenue and on the west by the John C. Lodge Expressway (Figure 8). The corridor projects a negative image. To many, the Cass Corridor means prostitution, drug addiction, and skid row. Crime is a serious problem, with homicide,

burglary, and arson relatively commonplace. Housing conditions in the area are among the worst in Detroit. There is an increasing number of abandoned and deteriorated buildings, many occupied by rats. Essential services such as health care and garbage collection are inadequate and appear to be worsening.

There is another side to the story, however. The Cass Corridor is home for about 20,000 people. The majority are poor, with 32.1 percent of families reporting incomes of less than $4,000 in 1969. Many are old, with almost 20 percent of the population sixty-five years of age or over, (compared with 11 percent for the city). Furthermore, many of the people are long time residents and have developed a strong sense of community identity. The area contains a varied ethnic mix. Southern whites are the dominant group, with Third Avenue frequently referred to in the recent past as "The Tennessee Valley" and "Little Kentucky." Cass Avenue is the home of Detroit's small Chinatown, a community displaced by urban renewal from its original location on Michigan Avenue close to downtown. A large black population is housed largely in a public housing project in the southwestern portion of the corridor. Other minorities include American Indians, Indians, Pakistanis, Philipinos, and Koreans, many of whom are students at the Detroit Institute of Technology or employed in the nearby Medical Center.

The character of the Cass Corridor has changed dramatically since the turn of the century, when it was known as "Piety Hill." In 1900 the Cass Corridor consisted of costly,

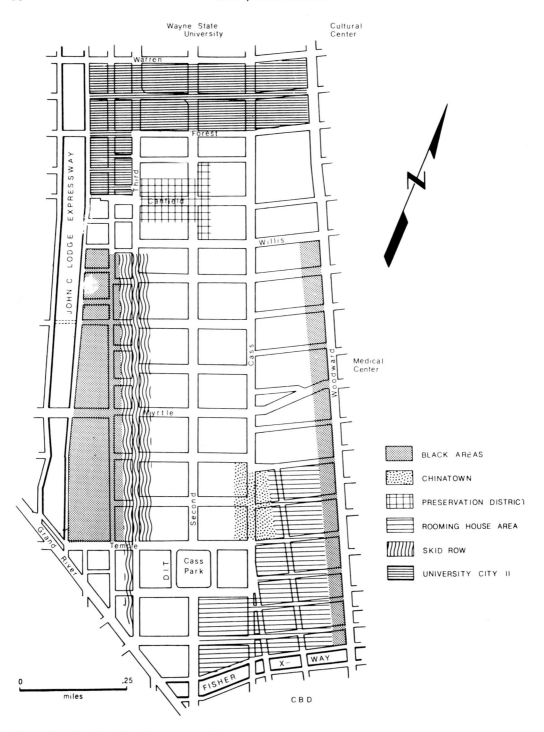

Figure 8. The Cass Corridor community.

durable single family residences housing De- troit's well-to-do. Rapid growth in the auto- mobile industry during the early years of the twentieth century resulted in major changes along Woodward Avenue. By the 1920s these streets, in a three mile strip extending north from Grand Circus Park, had become the center of the city's automobile sales. As more people flocked to Detroit, wealthy families in the Cass Corridor moved out and were replaced by middle and lower income people. Old resi- dences were subdivided into apartments and flats. Many newcomers found accommodation in the numerous apartment hotels that had been built in the area. Similar pressures were placed on the corridor's housing stock during World War II, when an estimated 200,000 white southerners came to Detroit looking for work. Increasingly the corridor became an area of apartments and rooming houses. Thus, up to the end of World War II, changes throughout the Cass Corridor were associated with (1) a changeover from residential use to commercial use along the major arteries, and (2) the sub- division of residential units and the construc- tion of high density units elsewhere.

In the last two decades a different force has left its mark on the area. Change has become associated with renewal, including freeway construction, institutional expansion, and ur- ban renewal. During the 1950s the John C. Lodge Expressway was built, cutting a north- south swath separating the Trumbull com- munity to the west from the Cass Corridor to the east. Later in the 1960s, the construction of the Fisher Freeway had a similar dismembering effect in the southern portions of the corridor. Other areas have been affected by both direct and indirect effects associated with institu- tional expansion. To the north renewal has been largely synonymous with the growth of Wayne State University, to the east with the development of a medical complex, and to the south with the anticipated extension of the Detroit Institute of Technology. Moreover, urban renewal projects in the central city, particularly those associated with downtown renewal in the fifties, have caused a spillover of population into the corridor. Thus, for the past two decades, and still today, conditions in the Cass Corridor are affected, and often determined, by different forms of renewal. Today, the legacy of those two decades is seen clearly throughout the corridor.

Renewal Processes in the Cass Corridor

The renewal process in the Cass Corridor takes on many forms and incorporates a variety of interacting processes. The most significant are associated with the expansionist policies of the educational, medical, and cultural institutions that abut the corridor on three sides.

Probably the most striking example of in- stitutional expansion is Wayne State University which, in its growth from a small city college to a state university, has acquired large tracts of community land and property. The uni- versity's expansion was slow until the late 1950s, but, in 1959, the Federal Housing Act made it easier for institutions of higher learning to expand. Land costs were reduced, the ability to acquire more land became easier, and costs were met by city and federal moneys. A plan for university growth was drawn up that was to proceed in five phases involving 304 acres. The project was labeled "University City." The first phase of the project, University City I, went ahead as scheduled, and by 1968 a forty acre area housing over 3,000 people had been replaced by a large physical education complex. In 1966 a law was enacted that pre- vented any urban renewal project from proceed- ing without citizen approval and involvement However, much damage had already been done through the University City area simply by the announcement of the 1959 renewal plan.

The second phase of the University City project involved property in both the Cass Corridor and the adjacent Trumbull commu- nity. Scheduled clearance was interrupted by a coalition of community organizations, whose injunction eventually was upheld by the courts. During the long interval, however, many home- owners had departed, maintenance on houses and apartment buildings had lapsed, and city purchases of property had continued. A com- munity plan was drawn up for this area, but little has been implemented. The present land- scape comprises vacant land, demolished houses, boarded-up houses, and a scattering of resi- dences where residents have remained.

Another phase of the University City proj- ect lies south of the university between Wood- ward and the Lodge Expressway. Much of this is now owned by the university, but existing functions remain until university development catches up. These functions include mixed university uses and rental apartments and houses on which few long term improvements are being made. Last, a large area in the northern part of the Cass Corridor is outside the University City project boundaries, but its condition is determined by the possibilities of university expansion. That condition is characterized by uncertainty and property neglect on the one hand, and the speculative ventures of many landowners on the other.

In sum, university expansion has had an adverse impact upon the Cass Corridor. The process has been slow and land acquisition piecemeal. During the long period involved, neighborhoods have deteriorated, houses have been abandoned, and life for remaining residents has become increasingly difficult. A sample quote from *The Community Reporter* indicates some of the difficulties:

> As property value declines so does property taxes, and with that city services. The residents of University City II were finding that they were no longer getting the police protection they once got. Houses are vacated and not boarded up or demolished, much less rehabilitated or replaced. Insurance went up sky-high or was denied altogether. And garbage pick-up and DPW services . . . were unreliable, or almost non-existent.

Wayne State University's expansion has been paralleled by that of other large institutions in and near the corridor. The Detroit Medical Center, comprising 240 acres immediately east of Woodward, is not in the Cass Corridor. However, the "spillover" of its population, which dropped from 85,000 in 1950 to about 20,000 in 1970, has had an indirect impact upon the corridor. Finally, the Detroit Institute of Technology moved into its present location near Cass Park on the southern edge of the area when the S.S. Kresge Company donated its office facility in the mid-1960s. Since that time, there has been some expansion into adjacent streets; the movement of students, many from overseas, into nearby residences; and considerable speculation in anticipation of future growth.

The renewal process has intensified many social problems throughout the Cass Corridor. Detroit's skid row, removed from its previous Michigan Avenue location by a renewal project of the 1950s, has migrated northward into the corridor and now is centered along Third Avenue between Temple and Selden avenues. Changes in occupancy have taken place as buildings in and near renewal areas deteriorated. Often, this meant that former occupants were replaced by alcoholics, drug addicts, prostitutes, and the physically and mentally disabled. Health problems have been compounded. The corridor has one of the highest tuberculosis rates in the country. Arson and crime have increased. All of those social problems have had an adverse affect upon family life and neighborhood stability even in the sounder residential streets.

These social problems have led to another kind of institutional expansion in the Cass Corridor. Social agencies, such as the Salvation Army, Goodwill Industries, Missionary Workers, and Mariner's Inn, and many church missions, have proliferated throughout the area. Though small scale in comparison with the massive public institutions that have been described, their cumulative impact is great. First, they are located throughout the corridor, quite often in what otherwise are residential areas. Second, they expand by taking over adjacent property, forcing residents to move. Third, their presence attracts greater numbers of the socially maladjusted into the area, thus perpetuating the need for their own existence and expansion. *The Community Reporter* reflects the feelings of many residents:

> The Salvation Army does provide many services for needy people. But it is too bad that while they offer those services they are also causing problems within the community. They have admitted that this is not the best place for their programs, but at the same time it is the only place that the "professional do-gooders" and politicians will let them have their building.

As if to justify the fears of many local residents, it was recently announced that the Salvation Army was planning a $3.4 million expansion program, much of it scheduled for the Cass Corridor.

Renewal has led to much speculative activity in the Cass Corridor. For example, university growth has meant an increased demand for student housing. Much of the area between Forest and Canfield is occupied by students. Many realtors and individual entrepreneurs have bought property, fixed it up, and turned out previous residents to accommodate students. Greater profits are realized. First, housing can be subdivided, and rents can be raised when two or more students share a single unit. Second, students—either because of family resources, part time employment, or student financial-aid programs—generally have more financial resources than many community residents, particularly the aged. Similar speculative ventures have occurred in the eastern sections of the Cass Corridor as a result of the growth of the medical complex. In sum, speculation resulting from the renewal process has caused resentment and hardship for many corridor residents.

One unusual form of renewal has had an impact upon a restricted part of the Cass Corridor. West Canfield Avenue between Second and Third avenues, a block of Victorian homes, has been designated a historic preservation district, and work is underway to restore the appearance and charm of what existed almost a century ago. Departments of the city, state, and the federal government have committed funds and facilities for the project. There has been some "rub-off" upon nearby areas as a few buildings on adjacent streets are now being restored in a similar manner. In spite of the limited scope of the whole development and its apparent value to the area, there have been unexpected results. Many local community residents regard the development as a factor that forces up property taxes, attracts middle class professionals into the area, and is a further threat to displace them from their homes.

In sum, the different forms of renewal have conditioned events and the nature of the landscape in the Cass Corridor for a period of twenty years. In some cases, the effects of the renewal processes have been direct—as, for example, where homes are torn down to be replaced by an institutional structure. More often they are indirect. Renewal has been a catalyst stimulating a set of other processes and incorporating a series of elements many of which at first glance have little connection with the renewal process.

The renewal processes operating in the Cass Corridor are perceived in different ways by the many persons who are involved in or affected by those processes. Clearly those perceptions depend upon the outlooks of the individuals involved. Generally, however, those individual viewpoints tend to reflect the divergence of two conflicting sets of interests—those of the community and those of institutional development. The former are the Cass Corridor residents and a number of community-based organizations that represent them. The latter are the institutional and governmental interests engaged in the renewal process.

Most Cass Corridor residents are involved in day-to-day questions of survival. Residents who have been in the community for a number of years have experienced or witnessed the direct effects of renewal. Many have been turned out of their homes. Others have seen their neighborhoods outlined in abstract "plans" formulated by outside organizations. Although the situation has improved with recent urban renewal legislation, the injustices and insensitivities of the past are not easily forgotten. Actions of the city, the university, and other institutions, no matter how sound, are viewed with suspicion, and as threats to the community.

Through the years, a host of organizations, official and unofficial, have been formed to represent the views of the community. The Citizens Governing Board (CGB), made up of elected representatives from various sections of the corridor, is the link with the Model Neighborhood Agency of which the Cass Corridor is a part. This board must approve federal programs before they can be implemented. The Citizens District Council (CDC), a product of urban renewal legislation, was active in opposing early university plans for expansion, and has developed alternative plans based on community involvement. The Peoples Area Development Corporation (PADCO) was incorporated as an independent, nonprofit development corporation to plan the physical development of the corridor in accordance with the Demonstration Cities Act of 1966. PADCO's role was advisory, to give expression to the needs and aspirations of its citizens. Although a detailed plan and inventory were drawn up, it is questionable whether their plan will be used. The United Community Housing Coalition has been concerned with the education and legal rights of tenants. Among a number of unofficial groups, the People Concerned About Urban Renewal (PCAUR) was at one time effective in countering aspects of the university's expansion plans. The local newspaper, *The Community Reporter,* has played an important role in alerting residents to events that might have an effect on their lives. Finally, the community churches have sponsored a variety of welfare and information programs. In total, these various organizations have met with considerable success. For example, they have caused Wayne State University to change its original plan of low-rise buildings incorporating larger expanses of land to one favoring high-rise development. Probably more important, they have fostered a notable degree of community cohesion. Although the efforts of these various community groups often appear trivial compared to those of the large scale organizations that they oppose, their cumulative efforts have not been in vain.

The institutional and governmental viewpoint is quite different. Those interests view the renewal process as a step toward the revival of the central city. This viewpoint is bolstered by the ongoing developments of the downtown Renaissance Center, and the extension of the Medical and Cultural centers east of Woodward. The New Center and the Burroughs Corporation administrative center complete what is hoped to be one giant institutional and business complex straddling Woodward Avenue from downtown to Grand Boulevard. The institutional attitude toward the plight of Cass Corridor residents has long been one of unconcern. This attitude is slowly changing. Wayne State University is reformulating some long range goals, and shows signs of recognizing community interests.

These divergent interests are brought into focus in the dichotomous outlook concerning the Cass Corridor's future. The resident sees his neighborhood and the corridor in general as a stage manipulated by vested power interests over which he himself has no control. The institutional and renewal interests see their role as revitalizing the central city. Clearly the needs of both groups could be accommodated with the proper attitudes and planning. In the foreseeable future, such accommodation appears most unlikely. Whatever the resolution, however, the effects of renewal processes are clearly outlined on the Cass Corridor landscape. It is appropriate to examine the spatial variation of those effects throughout the study area.

Spatial Variation of Renewal Processes in the Cass Corridor

Renewal processes have had a marked impact upon the corridor's population, which declined from 37,456 in 1950, to 24,113 in 1960, to 19,136 in 1970 (Figure 9). In the 1950–1960 decade some of this loss reflected postwar suburban migration, but much was caused by university expansion and the construction of the John C. Lodge Freeway. The northern part of the corridor showed the greatest losses (68.4 and 49.1 percent respectively) over the decade. The central part of the corridor had the smallest loss. The two northern tracts also had a sharp decline during the 1960–1970 decade, again because of university expansion. During

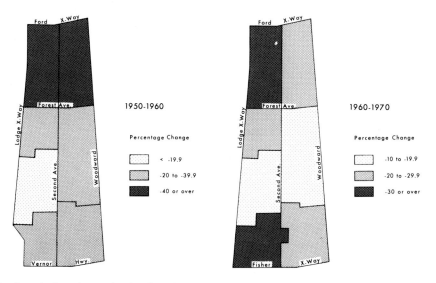

Figure 9. Population change in the Cass Corridor, 1950–1970.

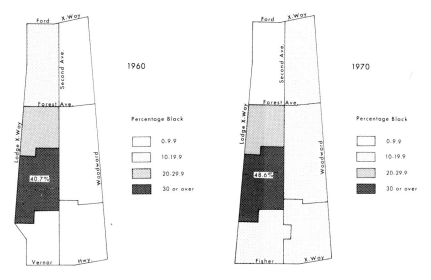

Figure 10. Black population change following urban renewal in the Cass Corridor, 1960-1970.

this decade the construction of the Fisher Free-way caused the population in the two southern tracts to decrease by 32.6 and 24.4 percent respectively. Again, tracts in the middle of the corridor had the smallest population losses. Thus, the pattern of population decline might be considered a contraction on all sides brought about by renewal processes surrounding the corridor.

Renewal has changed the racial composition of the corridor (Figure 10). In 1950 blacks comprised only 2.3 percent of the total population. In no census tract did they exceed 5 percent. Beween 1950 and 1960 the black population increased to 17.8 percent of the total, largely due to the construction of the E.J. Jeffries public housing project in the southwest section of the corridor. The tract that contains this project grew from 1.7 to 40.7 percent black over the decade. Between 1960 and 1970 the black population of the corridor increased to 24.2 percent. Increases in the three tracts bordering Woodward Avenue were related to the demolition of the virtually all-black Detroit Medical Center project area immediately east of Woodward. A decrease in the proportion of blacks in the two northwest tracts of the corridor likely reflects that blacks were affected more directly by the demolition program.

The effects of renewal upon residential stability are indicated in Figure 11, which shows for 1960 and 1970, the number of people who

were living in the same housing five years earlier. In 1960 the northern- and southern-most tracts displayed the greatest instability. Turnover in the north reflected the large student population. In the southwest section of the corridor, turnover was associated with skid row transiency and the opening up of the Jeffries housing project. In the southeast, it reflected aged and skid row populations living in rooming houses. The two central tracts were again the most stable. The same basic pattern was manifest in 1970, with increased stability in the tract containing the housing project. Thus, like the pattern of population decline, residential stability patterns show the encroachment on all sides upon the more stable central area.

Land ownership patterns illustrate the effects of institutional expansion as well as the speculative activities associated with anticipated change (Figure 12). Between 1960 and 1973 the most striking change was the decline in the amount of property owned by individuals, and a corresponding increase in that held by educational institutions, realtors and investment brokers, and large corporations. In the northern part of the corridor, particularly north of Forest Avenue, there was an increase in property owned by the university and the city of Detroit. South of the Wayne State renewal area, in a section bounded by Forest, Willis, Third and Cass avenues, realtors and investment corporations are holding large tracts of land. In

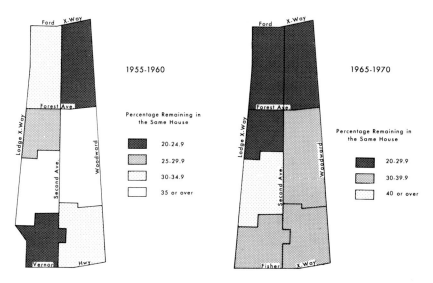

Figure 11. Population turnover in the Cass Corridor, 1955–1960 compared to 1965–1970.

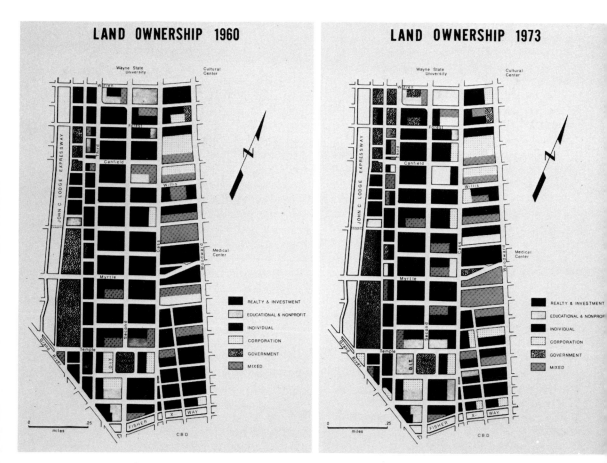

Figure 12. Land ownership in the Cass Corridor community, 1960 and 1973.

the southern part of the corridor, particularly south of Temple, increasing amounts of land are owned by educational institutions and investment companies, reflecting the presence, expansion, and anticipated additional development of the Detroit Institute of Technology. The increase in the amount of property owned by brokers and large corporations between Woodward Avenue and Cass Avenue, particularly between Canfield and Myrtle, was influenced by a proposed development plan incorporating the preservation of Orchestra Hall. In sum, elements associated with institutional expansion have brought about a profound change in the composition and pattern of land ownership in the Cass Corridor. Again, those changes are most pronounced on the outermost edges of the corridor, particularly in the northern and eastern sections, and to a lesser degree to the south.

Certain types of social agencies, such as Salvation Army missions, tend to concentrate in particular areas, but the agencies in general are well distributed throughout the corridor. Thus, unlike that of large institutions, the impact of social agencies upon adjacent residential areas comes from within the corridor, rather than from the edges.

Comparison of housing conditions between 1971 and 1974 indicates that distinct changes have taken place, many of which might be attributed to renewal (Figure 13). As might be expected, conditions in the university renewal area had deteriorated during the period. Likewise, a marked deterioration occurred along Third and Fourth avenues as far north as Canfield. On Third Avenue this represented an extension of skid row conditions, whereas on Fourth this deterioration appears to reflect a physical and psychological isolation from more viable residential areas east of Third. Elsewhere, declining housing conditions are

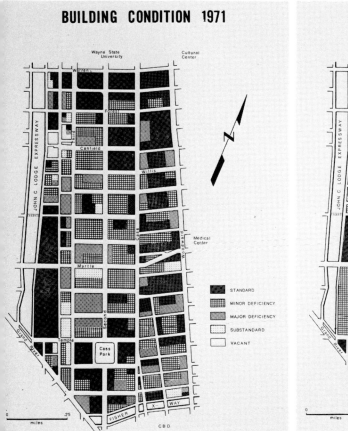

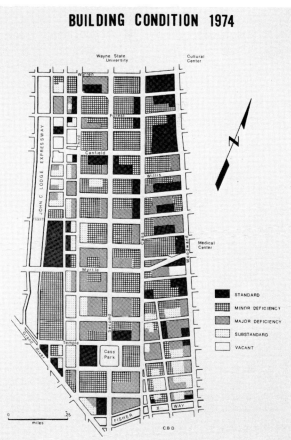

Figure 13. Condition of buildings in the Cass Corridor community, 1971 and 1973.

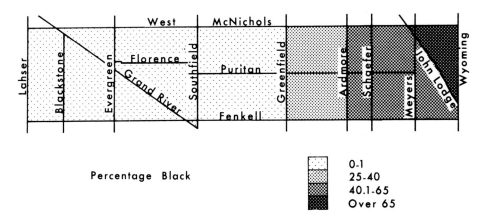

Figure 14. Northwest Detroit, black population in 1970. Source: Robert Sinclair, "Ghetto Expansion and the Urban Landscape," *Wiener Geographische Schriften, Festschrift Leopold G. Scheidel,* vol. 2 (1975).

related to stillborn urban renewal projects, the takeover of property by the Detroit Board of Education, and, in the southeast of the corridor, the deterioration of hotel-like quarters inhabited by old and poor individuals.

These different spatial patterns give a clear picture of what is happening within the Cass Corridor. To a large degree that picture is one of deterioration or of instability resulting from speculation about the future. Many of these patterns show the influence of surrounding renewal projects that are shrinking the viable community into a contracting residential core. There is little evidence in those patterns of a "renewal" in the conditions of Cass Corridor residents.

Like many other neighborhoods in the Detroit inner city, the Cass Corridor is subjected to forces of change, many associated with the renewal process. These forces are complex and incorporate a multitude of interrelated elements. They have resulted in hardship and conflict, and have left much of the corridor in a state of physical deterioration. In 1973, there is little indication of a resolution of the conflicts described here, and little overall understanding of the complex interrelationships associated with the forces of change. There is even less indication of a consensus concerning the corridor's future. This frustration and uncertainty allow the elements of conflict and decay to feed upon themselves and become increasingly worse.

RACIAL CHANGE IN NORTHWEST DETROIT

Northwest Detroit refers to a one mile wide strip extending five miles in an east-west direction between Wyoming and Lahser roads (Figure 14). The greater part of this strip is in the Detroit Middle Zone, but conditions west of the Southfield Freeway are more like those of the Suburban Area of Radial Development. Northwest Detroit currently is undergoing racial change, and the strip exhibits all aspects of that change. The change is associated with the overall northwesterly expansion of Detroit's black population, which has been such a dominant trend during the last two decades.

Traditionally, the northwest Detroit area has had an aura of well-being. Built during the late 1920s and 1930s, the area has been one of solid middle and upper income brick homes on quiet, tree-lined streets. Those streets were crossed at one mile intervals by major arteries, which provided both commercial facilities and excellent access to downtown Detroit and other parts of the city. The area's public and parochial schools had an outstanding reputation, churches were a source of local pride, and city services were excellent. Although the population of 51,113 in 1960 represented a diversity of occupations, incomes, and backgrounds, it was marked by a high degree of residential stability and a common sense of well-being. Among the many neighborhoods in northwest Detroit, two stand out as distinctive. Between Southfield and Evergreen is the prestigious Rosedale Park, inhabited by wealthy professionals, businessmen, and many Detroit civic leaders. In the extreme southwest is the old lower income community of Brightmoor, still dominated by poorly built wooden frame houses, and a cheap, deteriorated commercial strip along Fenkell Avenue.

In the past decade the long-standing residential stability of the area has been affected by a complex of forces associated with racial change. The black proportion of the population increased from less than 1 percent (fifteen persons) in 1960 to 24 percent (12,159 persons) in 1970. In the early 1960s the effects of racial transition were confined to the east and southeast edges of the area, the direction from which black expansion has taken place. By the end of the decade the prospect of racial change had been accepted in all but the westernmost parts of the area, and subsequent development has been conditioned by this fact.

The Process of Racial Change in Northwest Detroit

The steady influx of black population into northwest Detroit since the middle 1960s has been accompanied by white outmigration, so that the term racial succession best describes the process. Because this white suburban movement has involved many families with school age children, the present white population shows a higher than average proportion of older persons, childless couples, and civil servants tied to the city of Detroit by residence requirements. White families still move into some parts of the area, but they have not made up for the numbers who have moved to the suburbs. Thus, there has been an unusual choice of housing for blacks who are able to afford it. Black expansion in the study area initially includes those of middle and upper income, including professionals, businessmen, and white and blue collar workers. However, after this initial black migration, pressures follow from inner city ghetto areas, as poorer blacks, often deprived of former residences by various renewal processes, move into areas already occupied by blacks. Often, wealthier blacks move outward again as additional housing becomes available. Thus, black expansion in the study area involves not only racial transition, but

also a form of succession within the black population.

One of the most important elements associated with the above changes is a series of problems in the area's schools. Partly these problems reflect the overall financial difficulties of the Detroit public school system, but local factors are also involved. First, the dramatic population turnover leads to imbalances in student numbers. Some schools temporarily have declining enrollments due to outward migration. Others are subject to severe overcrowding because incoming black families generally have larger numbers of school age children than the white families they replace. Second, black students, coming from poorer sections of the city, often have more limited educational backgrounds than children brought up in the local area. Finally, public schools have been the scene of violent racial conflicts, gaining national attention during one disturbance in 1969. These factors all have an effect upon the quality of public schools. Parochial schools also have been affected. Traditionally, Roman Catholic schools have played an important educational role in northwest Detroit, and they remain a stabilizing influence in the western sections of the study area (Figure 15). However, many parochial schools have closed, largely for financial reasons, so that persons desiring a parochial educational system have turned elsewhere. Overall, school problems have become one of the most important causes of instability within the study area, and one of the main stimulants to more rapid suburban migration.

A second element is an increase in crime. Crimes reported to the Detroit Police Department increased in the area from 1,324 in 1966, to 3,249 in 1970, to 4,131 in 1972. This increase involves a set of complex and apparently contradictory factors. Although "crime in the streets" is a citywide phenomenon, the greatest concentrations tend to be in slums and more blighted areas of the inner city. To some degree the spread of crime in northwest Detroit reflects (1) the spread of blighted, inner city conditions into parts of the study area, and (2) the instability of the transition process. The impact of increasing crime in the study area is great. Evidence of a violent crime induces thoughts of departure for those financially able to move—whether white in a racially

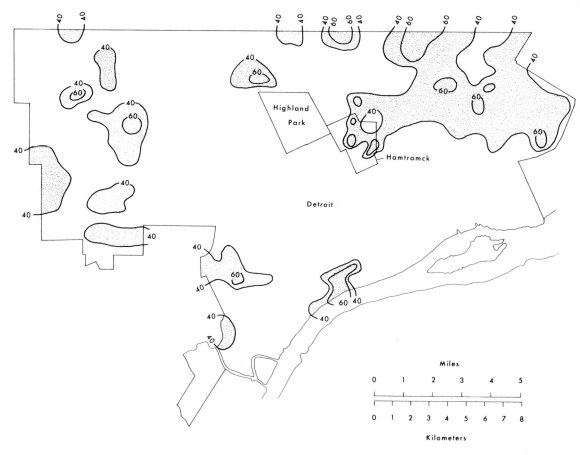

Figure 15. Percentage of elementary school children attending parochial schools in 1970.

changing neighborhood or black in a neighborhood undergoing the spread of blight. Moreover, the fear of crime, and responses to that fear—watchdogs, bricked-over windows, burglar alarms, metal screens, and empty streets—create an appearance of instability and have a further blighting effect upon a neighborhood.

There have been significant changes in northwest Detroit's commercial structure. The one time prosperous "Mile Roads" of the study area have experienced commercial decline, as local residents were attracted to suburban shopping malls, and as the customers replacing them have had less purchasing power. As a result there has been a decline in the quality of merchandise and services; the introduction of different functions, merchandise, and merchandising habits; and an overall advance of neglect and decay. Streets in the eastern part of the study area take on aspects of the inner city ghetto. Many stores are empty or boarded up. Screens,

padlocks, and security guards are part of the local retail scene. Moreover, many of those indexes of commercial decline are found in advance of other aspects of change, in areas otherwise untouched by blight. The psychological impact upon adjacent residential areas is assumed to be considerable.

The rapidly changing situation in the study area incorporates many elements that have no original relationship with the racial change process, but that become an integral part of that process with the passage of time. One such element is associated with the HUD house problem, which has had such detrimental effects in Detroit. The circumstances leading to the presence of such homes have already been described. These circumstances are accentuated in areas of instability, and their evidence is marked within the study area. Many streets in black and mixed neighborhoods are pockmarked with vacant homes, some falling into disrepair, and all presenting an unkempt appearance. The presence of one or more such houses on any street is detrimental to adjacent properties. Potential residents are turned away. Often the result is to hasten the approach of residential blight. Another such element is a general reduction in city services, brought on in the last decade by a consistent decrease in city revenues, with an accompanying decline in civil service morale. The reduction is not so marked in the western part of the study area, largely due to the greater political influence of its residents. In the eastern section, where political influence is not so great and population instability has placed greater demands upon limited services, the effects of the reduction are pronounced. A third and unexpected element is the presence of Dutch Elm disease. A pleasing feature of northwest Detroit is the presence of tall elm trees, which line almost every residential street and blend with brick homes to provide a residential landscape of great beauty. In recent years many of those trees have been afflicted with Dutch Elm disease and have been cut down, leaving many front yards stark and void. The destruction of this element of the cityscape has changed the appearance of some areas, such that it is difficult to distinguish this from other indexes of blight.

In sum, the complex of elements described above has had a blighting effect upon the landscape of the study area. Blight, in promoting residential instability, becomes itself part of the racial transition process, even though many of the contributing elements originally were independent of that process. Blight is not easily eradicated when the racial transition process is complete. Indeed, because the initial expansion of black occupance often is followed by a subsequent movement of poorer blacks, bringing problems of the inner city ghetto, blighted conditions have tended to increase.

Several agents are consciously involved in directing or controlling black expansion in the study area. One is the real estate industry. Certain real estate companies clearly have manipulated the racial transition process for personal gains, which include not only commissions accruing from rapid housing turnover, but also profits made by buying homes at panic rates from departing whites and selling at higher rates to incoming blacks. There have been case examples of the well-known panic-promoting tactics associated with blockbusting. Within the study area at least two lawsuits are underway charging real estate companies with designating "territories" inside which, by agreement, sales to blacks (or whites respectively) are discouraged. The interest of realtors in the transition process is marked by concentrations of short-lived real estate offices along the study area's business streets. Although the more overt practices have become subdued in recent years under the pressures of city ordinances, local community organizations, and press publicity, the real estate element still plays an important role in determining the nature and pattern of black expansion in the study area.

A second and countering agent is the local community councils, which have become the foci of efforts to combat the more deleterious aspects of change in the study area. Activities of these councils include pressuring city government to change zoning laws and improve services, obtaining funds for school improvements, organizing block clubs, and uniting citizen support against real estate blockbusting and the increase in HUD housing. Probably more important, they have fostered much community cohesion. It is no coincidence that most organizations correspond to and take their names from the traditional units of local loyalty in the area, namely the primary and secondary school districts.

As might be expected, the changing situation in northwest Detroit has been the source of conflicts and tensions. The most dramatic type of conflict is racial, beginning with white antipathy toward incoming blacks, and ending with black resentment toward white persons remaining in otherwise black areas. Detroit newspapers have described extreme cases of cross burnings on lawns of incoming black families, as well as harrassment of elderly white couples by black youths. Nevertheless, the most violent confrontations have occurred in the area's schools.

Other types of conflict are less dramatic. They include those divergences in outlooks, perceptions, and responses that tend to be characteristic of changing areas. These conflicts tend to vary throughout the study area. In the rapidly changing central part of the study area, middle and upper middle income blacks, who were early migrants into the area, often resent the later arrival of poorer blacks. Those wealtheir blacks tend to be most conscious of the blight, commercial decline, and deterioration in services that have taken place in much of the study area. Often, their response is to move farther west within the study area.

The white resident of this central area also has a distinct set of attitudes. He is fully aware of the ongoing transition processes and is quite convinced that the area where he lives will be predominantly black within the next few years. Like the middle income blacks of the same area, he is conscious of the blighting processes that are spreading within the area. Moreover, he is able to compare conditions today with those of the somewhat nostalgic past. For the most part, he considers it almost inevitable that he will move out of the area within the next five years. Unlike his black counterpart in the same area, his move is likely to be to a suburb, most likely Farmington, Southfield, or Redford Township.

The wealthier white resident in the western part of the study area has a somewhat different attitude. He also is aware of the changes taking place, and anticipates some racial change within his own neighborhood. However, he tends to believe that the more adverse elements associated with racial change are not inevitable, and that change will not necessarily affect his neighborhood's general stability. Generally, his attitude toward increased integration is more optimistic, and he is less inclined to consider moving from the area. This attitude brings to the fore one other aspect of conflict—namely, the conflict between certain elements of the real estate industry and the organizations attempting to preserve neighborhood stability. It is predominantly in the western part of the study area that this last-named conflict is to be found today.

Though less clear cut than the direct racial confrontations in the eastern part of the study area, these last-named conflicts in the western area have much meaning. They imply an awareness of the blighting elements that have accompanied racial transition, a belief that such elements are not inevitable, a recognition of the need for community efforts to counter those elements, and a realization among many that those efforts must include a considerable amount of integration. At the same time, the very existence of this realization tends to create a "self-fulfilling prophecy" of things to come. Conflicts within the western part of the area are

symptoms of an early stage of the racial transition process, just as the more direct confrontations farther east exemplify a later stage. The outcome of those earlier conflicts might well determine the future of the western parts of the study area.

In summary, racial change in northwest Detroit involves a large number of diverse elements, many of which have no original connection with the racial change process. In time those elements become closely identified with the process and bring about conditions that tend to bring about its continuation. It is appropriate to examine the spatial variation of those conditions throughout the study area.

Spatial Variation of the Racial Change Process in Northwest Detroit

The status of racial transition in northwest Detroit in 1970 is shown in Figure 14. The easternmost square mile has experienced almost complete racial turnover, with all census tracts more than 70 percent black. In the next three square miles the black population comprises more than 50 percent, 25 percent, and 2 percent respectively. In the remaining western areas the percentage is less than one.

The recency of population turnover is illustrated in Figure 16, which expresses the percentage of 1970 residents who were living in the area in 1965. In most of the western part of the area this percentage was between sixty-five and seventy-five, indicating a relatively high degree of stability. Toward the east this percentage declines to forty east of Greenfield and to twenty-five in the two easternmost square miles. This means that population turnover in eastern areas was as much as 75 percent within a five year period. The 1960–1970 population change map indicates aspects of the family structure of new residents (Figure 17). The eastern area shows a considerable population increase, as black families not only filled vacancies created by departing whites, but did so with larger families and consequently greater population densities. With one exception, no significant population change is discerned elsewhere in the study area.

The pattern of active racial turnover in early 1973 is suggested by a map of real estate listings (Figure 18). An east-west profile of numbers of houses for sale resembles a wave, with its crest in the central square mile, be-

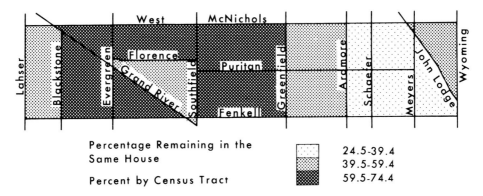

Figure 16. Population turnover in northwest Detroit, 1965-1970.

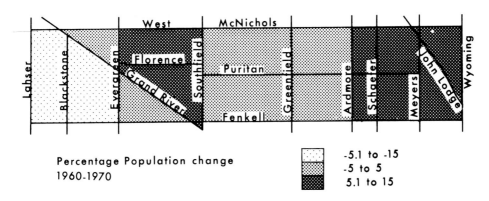

Figure 17. Population change in northwest Detroit, 1960-1970.

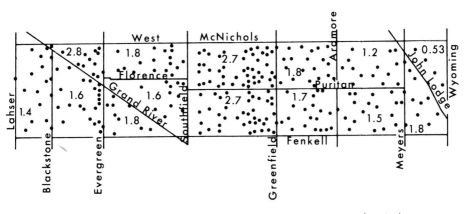

Figure 18. Northwest Detroit, Houses for Sale February 1973. Source: Robert Sinclair, "Ghetto Expansion and the Urban Landscape," *Wiener Geographische Schriften, Festschrift Leopold G. Scheidel,* vol. 2 (1975).

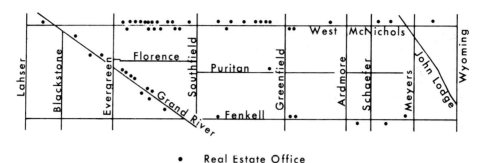

• Real Estate Office

Figure 19. Real estate offices in northwest Detroit, October 1973. Source: Robert Sinclair, "Ghetto Expansion and the Urban Landscape," *Wiener Geographische Schriften, Festschrift Leopold G. Scheidel,* vol. 2 (1975).

tween Greenfield and Southfield. To the west, in front of the wave, the "for sale" density is half as great. To the east, behind the crest of the wave, the "for sale" density is also half as great, but only in the first square mile. It declines to less than 30 percent after the first square mile.

The relationship between the pattern of houses for sale and that of real estate offices is revealing. Reference has been made to the east-west movement of short-lived real estate offices along the commercial arteries of the study area. Figure 19 shows the location of such offices during the summer of 1973. Practically no real estate offices are to be found in the western two miles. Offices in the eastern two miles are relatively few, about three per mile. The greatest concentration, ten and sixteen per mile, is found in the two square miles between Greenfield and Evergreen, closer to the area of active turnover. However, the peak of this concentration is between Greenfield and Evergreen. This is one mile ahead of the area of active racial transition, in an area which remains predominantly white. The pat-

tern of real estate offices would seem to be a portent of other patterns of the future.

Quite a different pattern is shown in the map of housing in FHA mortgage default (Figure 20). In the two easternmost square miles the proportion of such houses is among the highest in the city, ranging from 3.7 to 7 percent. This proportion declines rapidly to the west, and becomes negligible throughout the remainder of the area. This general pattern is expressed more vividly in a map of vacant HUD homes (Figure 21). Virtually all such homes are in the easternmost two square miles. This area already has gone through the racial transition process, and has a relatively stable "for sale" situation. The chain of circumstances that led to mortgage defaults and the presence of vacant HUD homes appears to be initiated well after other change processes have taken place. It might be hypothesized that the rapid turnover of homes in the preceding period led to purchases by families who were unable to afford either home upkeep or mortgage payments. The backwash is the incidence of vacant HUD homes.

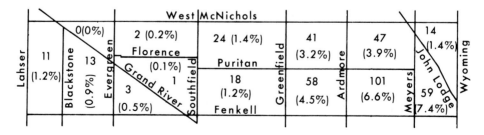

Figure 20. The number (and percentage) of each tract's houses in FHA (HUD) mortgage default, October, 1973, in northwest Detroit.

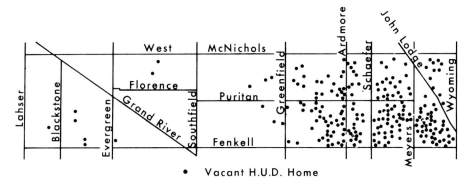

Figure 21. Vacant HUD houses, March 1973. Source: Robert Sinclair, "Ghetto Expansion and the Urban Landscape," *Wiener Geographische Schriften, Festschrift Leopold G. Scheidel*, vol. 2 (1975).

Patterns expressing commercial blight closely parallel those of housing default and vacancy. Figure 22 maps the vacancy status of stores and offices along main commercial arteries in the summer of 1973. The overwhelming concentration in the east is clear, where the percentage of vacancies on some streets is more than 40 percent. The vacancy count declines by more than one-half in the middle section, and with one minor exception becomes even lower in the western sections. Figure 23 maps the incidence of protective devices (iron screens, metal bars, bricked-in windows, etc.) on the windows of commercial structures. Again, the concentration in the east is apparent. The circumstances leading to commercial blight are initiated before and during the time of racial transition, but become more prevalent after the initial transition has taken place. The commercial condition in the easternmost square mile is akin to that in Detroit's inner city ghetto.

When the different patterns are considered in perspective, a further insight is gained into the complicated process of racial change. Each pattern varies from east to west. The patterns do not coincide, however. If the basic pattern is black-white occupancy change, then racial change in 1973 is concentrated in the middle square mile, between Greenfield and Southfield. Certain patterns, such as that of houses for sale, correspond to this basic pattern. Others, such as those for population, commercial blight, and housing vacancies, are con-

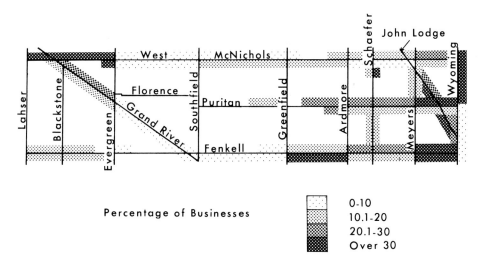

Percentage of Businesses

0-10
10.1-20
20.1-30
Over 30

Figure 22. Commercial vacancies in northwest Detroit, October 1973.

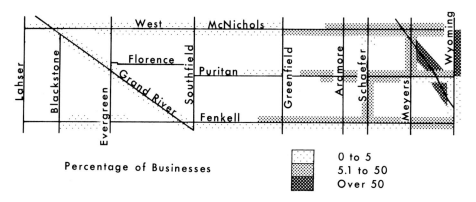

Figure 23. Incidence of storefront protective screens in northwest Detroit, October 1973.

centrated behind (to the east). Others, including the pattern of real estate offices, show an intensity well ahead (to the west) of the peak of racial transition. In sum, the process of racial change is not confined to the edge of racial transition. Conditions in large areas behind this edge reflect that this transition has taken place in the past. Conditions far in advance are underlain by the anticipation of that change.

Like many other areas of the city, our five mile strip of northwest Detroit in 1973 is a locale within which the complex forces associated with racial change are to be found. These forces already have had a profound impact upon large parts of the area. Whether that impact will be similar in the remainder of the area, and in other nearby areas, still is to be determined.

URBAN EXPANSION IN OAKLAND TOWNSHIP

Oakland Township is a standard thirty-six square mile survey township in northeastern Oakland County some thirty miles from downtown Detroit (Figure 24). Long exhibiting the features associated with the Zone of Rural Change, the township now appears destined to undergo the processes associated with direct urban expansion. That expansion comes from the south, an apparent continuation of the process that has engulfed Birmingham, Troy, Rochester, and Avon Township. Thus the elements involved are associated with the Zone of Radial Development.

Traditionally Oakland Township has de-

picted a prosperous rural landscape, on a rolling to hilly upland which is interrupted only in the southwest by the valley of Paint Creek and its tributaries. One of the county's earliest settled townships, it developed rapidly into an area of prosperous farmers concerned primarily with dairying and cattle raising. The agricultural scene has been enhanced by the presence of farming estates, owned by wealthy Detroit families, farmed by efficient year round managers and used by their owners as summer residences. Several families have turned their land holdings into game and wildlife preserves. Since the 1940s affluent nonfarm residents have appeared on the scene. Their arrival in the township might be considered part of a slow ongoing process, which has contributed to, rather than detracted from, a relatively harmonious symbiosis.

It is this symbiosis that has been disrupted by forces associated with urban expansion. Initially these forces were quite subtle. By the late 1960s the prospect of eventual urbanization had become accepted and the township's subsequent development was conditioned by this acceptance. Thus for more than six years the township has been in the shadow of urban expansion. It remains in this shadow, but today development seems so inevitable that the direct impact stage appears to be approaching.

The Urban Expansion Process in Oakland Township

Underlying all other aspects of the urban expansion process in Oakland Township is the steady influx of wealthy nonfarm persons. Those migrants are attracted by a beautiful

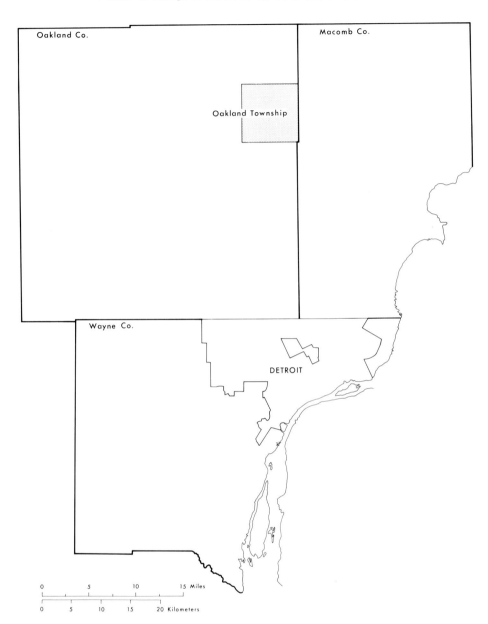

Figure 24. Oakland Township in Oakland County.

landscape, an open rural environment, and the opportunity for exclusive exurbanite living. Some have more specific desires, such as the proximity of reputable private schools, the presence of Oakland University, and even the opportunity to keep horses. For many, prestige is a factor. Automobile executives from the General Motors Tech Center and from Ford and Chrysler Corporations have established homes in the township. Professors and ad-

ministrators from Oakland University have been attracted there, as have persons in other professions. There is evidence of an outward "sifting" of families from Detroit's more prestigious communities, such as Birmingham, Bloomfield Hills, and the Grosse Pointes. The high socioeconomic status of Oakland Township's residents is indicated by the fact that 50 percent had incomes between $15,000 and $30,000 in 1970, with more than 12 percent earning more than $30,000. Almost 50 percent had college degrees, and over 20 percent had advanced degrees. In general, it is this category of resident that has accounted for the township's population growth, from about 1,000 in the 1950s, to 5,000 in 1970, to about 10,000 by 1975.

This population influx has been accompanied by basic changes in the township's farming structure. Most farmers in Oakland Township are in their late fifties and early sixties, and many are near retirement. Few of their children have chosen to continue farming, and dependable farm labor has become almost nonexistent. As a result, there has been a gradual decline in the more arduous, intensive, and long term types of farming—quite often a sequence from dairying, to meat animals, to cash crops, and in some places to idle land. Other factors have hastened the process. Farm equipment costs have become exorbitant. Equipment dealers and repairmen have left the local scene. The former agricultural and marketing infrastructure largely has disappeared. Finally, farming operations increasingly have been affected by "nuisances." These include well-known rural-urban problems like frightening livestock, treading on crops, stealing fruit, and throwing garbage; as well as more recent problems, such as the noise and environmental destruction caused by motor bikes in summer and snowmobiles in winter.

One element that has had a great impact upon farmers and nonfarm residents alike is the recent changes in property taxes. In the past few years three factors have combined to bring about what appear to be staggering tax increases. One is the rise accompanying higher land values as the township changed from a rural condition to one of anticipated urbanization. A second is increased millages caused by improved services and planned services (sewer interceptors, increased school populations, etc.). A third is the implementation of recent state regulations that all Michigan private property be assessed at 50 percent of appraised value. Any one of these factors might have been enough to influence decisions of residents and landowners. Occurring together, they have caused farmers to give up farming or move to other agricultural areas, estate owners to reduce or subdivide their property, and land speculators to sell land to developers much earlier than they normally would have.

One event has recently altered the pattern of urban expansion in the township. This is the construction of the Paint Creek sewer interceptor, which is scheduled to serve a district encompassing much of the southwest portion of the township. Normally such a utility is a synonym for suburban growth in the Zone of Rural Change, and the recent spate of real estate activity appears to verify the fact that this part of Oakland Township will be no exception. At the same time, the interceptor has generated great controversy within the township, bringing into focus many of the conflicting attitudes toward growth that are discussed later in this section.

The urban expansion process in Oakland Township is influenced directly and consciously by what might be termed the "development" component. This reflects the actions of decisionmakers who manipulate, convert, develop, and build upon land. The township shows evidence of the well-known complex of landowners, speculators, developers, builders, and managers, serviced by the activities of realtors, bankers, loan companies, insurance companies, lawyers, advertisers, and political pressure groups. At first glance the operations of this complex appear to be at an early stage in Oakland Township, in that the amount of subdivided land is small and scattered. Other factors indicate that the operation is further advanced. Virtually all land within the Paint Creek Sewer Interceptor District is in the hands of speculators or developers. Much land elsewhere in the township belongs to speculators, although often it is rented to local farmers. The development component shows a remarkable degree of external control. The traditional local real estate agent has long since been superseded by companies that have moved their main offices to Birmingham and Bloomfield Hills, and established branch offices in Troy, Rochester, and other suburbs. Development companies in the Paint Creek Sewer Interceptor District also are developing land throughout the Detroit region. Bankers, insurance companies, and law firms which service the developers operate from downtown Detroit or some well-established suburb. The overriding impression is that the development component comprises a well-organized, externally located decisionmaking complex. Today the operations of that complex are at an initial stage. Given the right circumstances, they might well proceed at an unexpectedly rapid pace.

As in any area of change, psychological factors have an influence on events in Oakland Township. One such factor might be termed the Avon Township syndrome. Although many residents of Oakland Township might not fully comprehend the ongoing expansion processes, they can readily observe the consequences of those processes in other suburbs. Often the very mention of such suburbs brings about a psychological reaction. The closest (visibly, physically, and psychologically) of those suburbs is the immediate neighbor to the south, Avon Township, which currently is undergoing the full impact of suburbanization. To many Oakland Township residents "growth" means what is taking place to the south. Whether such growth is viewed favorably (as it is by some) or with distaste (as it is by most), the vision of Avon Township looms large in the actions and decisions made in Oakland Township.

In recent years those actions and decisions have shown a considerable degree of organization. A relatively large proportion of the township's residents are highly educated; are interested in the township's future; and have professional competence in planning, government, and law. Cooperation has taken place among those residents. An outgrowth of this cooperation is the Oakland Township Association, a citizen's group that has actively influenced local government. As a result the township has adopted several unique conservation ordinances (soil and erosion control, wetlands, zoning, purchase of land for recreational purposes, etc.), is formulating a master plan, seeks the advice of county and metropolitan planners, and attempts to involve more residents in important township decisions. The association has become a model for similar citizens organizations throughout the state. The degree to which the Oakland Township Association will be able to control and direct future forces of growth in the township is uncertain. Today, however, the association plays a significant role in the township's development.

Almost inevitably the forces of change in Oakland Township have given rise to tensions and conflicts. Those conflicts are not only connected with the broad forces of urbanization that already have been described; they also include those differences in individual

human perceptions, responses, and opinions that crop up in situations of change. Clearly those differences stem from the particular characteristics and outlooks of individuals. Often, however, they tend to polarize around the divergent attitudes of two general groups of residents. One group comprises the recent immigrants—relatively young, with high incomes, living in wealthy subdivisions in the southern part of the township. The other includes the township's longtime residents—older, with large landholdings (farms or estates), but with relatively low annual incomes. This group lives largely in the middle and northern parts of the township.

The divergence between those two groups is expressed in their general perception of impending urbanization. The more recent subdivision resident is closer to, more experienced with, and has more information about the expansion processes taking place within the township. He tends to be more conscious of the indexes of decline in the rural environment. Most significantly, he observes on a firsthand, day-to-day basis the growth of adjacent Avon Township, and is more able to project the possibility of a similar growth pattern in Oakland Township. The long term resident farther north, though most concerned about increasing taxes and increasing nuisances, appears to be less aware of the deeper implications of the urban expansion process.

The divergence between the two groups can also be observed in their preferences for the township's future development and, more particularly, in the degree to which each group is willing to pay for those preferences. Certain preferences are universal. For example, virtually all Oakland Township residents profess a desire to preserve as much of an open, rural atmosphere as possible. Most residents oppose high density developments. Most prefer to continue traveling outside the township for commercial purposes rather than allowing commercial development within the township. Moreover, most residents show an expression of support for the efforts of the Oakland Township Association. However, opinions differ sharply between the two groups concerning how those preferences should be brought to fruition. The recently arrived subdivision residents favor immediate township purchase of land for future space needs and are willing to pay increased taxes for this purpose. The longtime residents tend to be opposed. Living in the more rural part of the township, the latter do not perceive the loss of open space to be so imminent. Moreover, their larger landholdings would subject them to undue taxation to pay for such purchases. These differences are closely associated with a more general divergence in attitude toward growth. Subdivision residents in the south wish to limit and control residential growth. Longtime residents are more amenable to growth. In sum, it is the newcomers who want fewer newcomers and who, as the longtime residents say, "want to be the very last persons to come into the township."

The resulting conflicts are many and varied. New subdivision residents want to retain the traditional rural "natural beauty" roads, are opposed to new subdivisions, and object to the idea of any industrial or commercial enterprise in the township. Their more northerly counterparts are more interested in sound road maintenance (they are more dependent on it), are not so opposed to new developments, and often see some type of industrial or commercial development as the only solution to soaring property taxes. These differences lead to a somewhat divergent attitude toward

planning. Newcomers are more likely to consult with county planning officials, to promote zoning ordinances, and to support activities of the Oakland Township Association. The longtime residents might show an overt interest, but inherently tend to be suspicious of any ordinance that might threaten their ability to make independent decisions.

In summary, urban expansion in Oakland Township involves a number of diverse and interacting elements. Ironically, many of those elements have no initial connection with the urban expansion process. Almost inevitably they become incorporated into the process and tend to hasten its progress. Certain conditions associated with the urban expansion process are to be observed on the township's landscape. It is appropriate to examine the spatial variation of those conditions.

Spatial Variation of the Urban Expansion Process in Oakland Township

The pattern of immigration into Oakland Township is illustrated by the location of residential subdivisions in the years 1956, 1964, and 1973 (Figure 25). In 1956 plotted land was found only around Cranberry Lake in the north

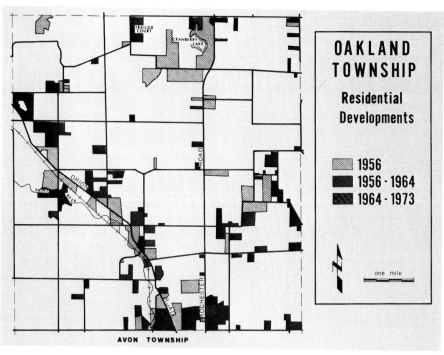

Figure 25. Oakland Township, residential subdivisions, 1956, 1964, 1973.

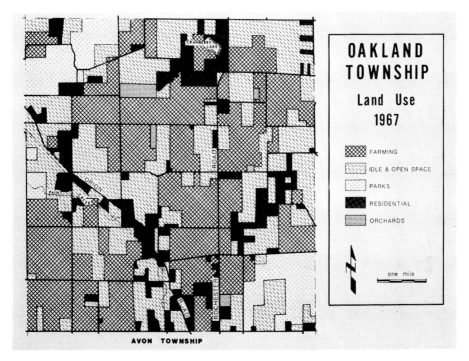

Figure 26. Oakland Township, land use, 1967.

of the township, where the development represented summer weekend cottages, along Orion Road overlooking the scenic Paint Creek Valley, and in a few small patches east of Rochester Road. By 1964 consolidation had taken place around all these nuclei, particularly along the Orion Road artery. Subdivision activity that has taken place since that time has been concentrated along Orion Road and more conspicuously in two sections in the southern part of the township along Orion, Livernois, and Rochester roads. It is in these two last named areas that most subdivision currently is taking place. Today the overall impression in all those residential areas is that of affluent exurbia, from the individual villas nestled in the hills overlooking Paint Creek Valley to the extensive landscaped subdivisions in the southern tiers, to the acreage estates with their horse farms found in other parts of the township. The one exception to this picture of affluence is a set of mobile homes in the far north, the township's concession to a federal regulation requiring some space in every community to be set aside for low income housing.

These residential subdivisions comprise only a small part of the township's total land use, as shown in 1967 and 1973 (Figures 26 and

27). More than five-sixths of Oakland Township is in two categories—farmland and idle open land. The remaining one-sixth is occupied mainly by public parks.

The largest farm acreages are found in a relatively compact area in the center of the township and in a smaller area to the southwest. Farming here, however, is a far cry from the prosperous dairying of the 1950s. Since that period it has changed, first to the raising of cattle and sheep for the local market, and later to the present emphasis on cash crops. These cash crops include hay for the townships 650 recreational horses as well as for ponies in the Detroit's Belle Isle Park, wheat for the mill in nearby Richmond, and corn for sale as feed for farmers farther to the north. By 1973 only one farmer had dairy cattle, while two pastured some beef cattle. The changing nature of farming is also marked by the increase in rented land, which even in 1967 comprised approximately half the farmland. Many farmers have found it more profitable to sell their land and rent it back from the new owners.

Farmland acreage is almost equaled by that of open or idle land. Open land is found throughout the township but is concentrated in the east, along the northern fringe, and in a

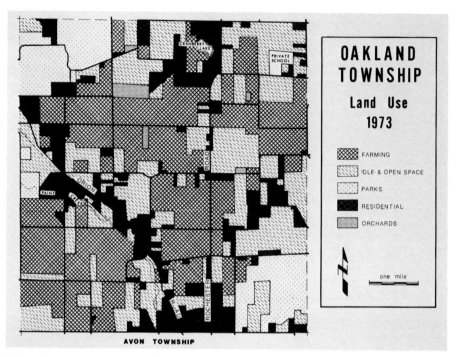

Figure 27. Oakland Township, land use, 1973.

broad belt on both sides of the Paint Creek Valley. Much of this land traditionally has been idle, comprising wetlands, forested land, and the preserves of private landowners who have chosen to keep their land in a relatively natural state. Oakland Township is exceptional in having only a small amount of the neglected, abandoned farmland that is so characteristic of other parts of the Zone of Rural Change. Thus, unlike other parts of that zone, the categories marked "idle and open" continue to have considerable aesthetic appeal. The particular nature of idle land in the township explains why there was no increase in that category between 1967 and 1973.

Perhaps the most revealing spatial pattern is that of land ownership, which can be examined by looking at the ownership categories of large land parcels in 1956, 1967, and 1973 (Figures 28, 29 and 30). In 1956 only a few parcels of land were in the hands of investors. Otherwise land was still owned by families who had been there for fifteen to one hundred years. By 1966 approximately 2,155 acres of land, largely in the center and southwest of the township, had been sold to investors, This corresponded closely with the rented farmland in the

1967 land use map. Between 1967 and 1973 the ownership pattern changed more dramatically, as a further 3,598 acres were sold to investors and 491 acres to developers. By the summer of 1973 few parcels remained in original hands, and the largest remaining parcel, a 750 acre farm, was up for sale.

To a remarkable degree the land ownership pattern explains the pattern of land use. The bulk of the farmland in Oakland Township is not in the hands of farmers, but is owned by investors who lease out their land (often to the original owners) until the time is right for selling (generally to developers). Much of the idle land is also in the hands of investors or developers. In 1973 the most notable ownership trend was the increase in direct purchases by developers and the shortened time span of investor-owned land, a trend prompted by recent tax increases. For example, the aforementioned 750 acre farm was being considered, not by an investor, but directly by a developer.

One of the most significant spatial patterns is that of land values. Although lack of specific information makes the construction of accurate land value maps impossible, local insights enable generalizations to be made. Those gen-

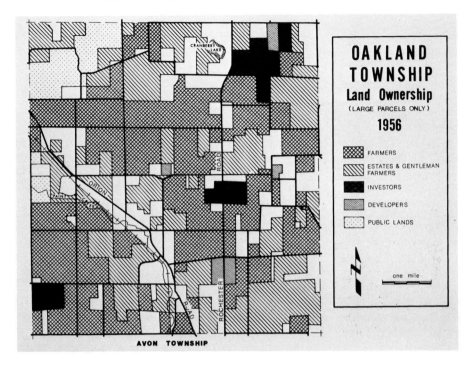

Figure 28. Oakland Township, land ownership, 1956.

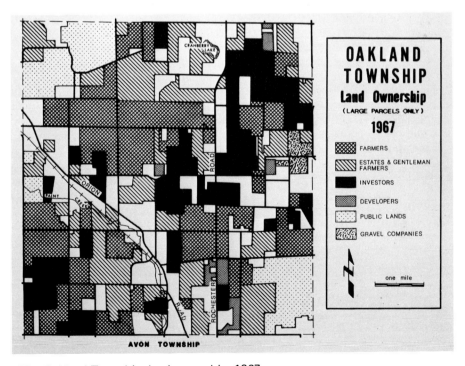

Figure 29. Oakland Township, land ownership, 1967.

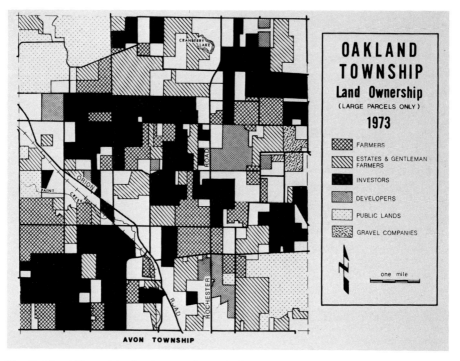

Figure 30. Oakland Township, land ownership, 1973.

eralizations are on two levels—namely, open land (both farmed and idle) and subdivided land. The status of open land is depicted easily. In 1960 farmland in Oakland Township sold for about $600 per acre. In 1967 this land had increased to $2,000 per acre and by 1973 the price was $5,000. Obviously such prices do not reflect the value for farming. The status of subdivided land also is easily portrayed. In 1973 half acre to one acre lots on spacious subdivisions sold for $10,000 and, in spots of particular scenic amenities, for $20,000. Such prices reflect the unique economic status of the township's residents. They also provide a clue to the future development of the township. Either future migrants into the township will continue to be among the wealthiest in the Detroit area, or parts of the township will give way to high density residential developments. Which of those two alternatives will prevail is perhaps the most important question facing Oakland Township.

When considered independently, each of these spatial patterns provides a clue to what is happening in Oakland Township. When the patterns are considered together and in per-

spective, an even clearer picture of the township begins to emerge. It is a picture underlain by the anticipation of change and determined by the uncertainty associated with that change. Like other parts of the Zone of Rural Change, Oakland Township in the mid-1970s had become a stage upon which the complex forces of urban expansion were beginning to impinge. Because of the township's particular socioeconomic status, the effects of those forces might well be different than in other parts of the Detroit system. To what degree it will be different cannot now be foreseen.

SUMMARY

The Cass Corridor, the northwest Detroit strip, and Oakland Township are small areas within the Detroit system that in the mid-1970s are affected by different forces of change. Despite the wide disparity among the three areas, and the different forces that are involved, there are elements of similarity in the three cases. Most apparent is the complexity of each situation. At the local level, forces of change involve a myriad of elements. Many of those elements have no initial connection with the basic process involved, but in time they are incorporated into the process and become integral parts of it. Each of the three situations also is characterized by conflict and instability, which extend well beyond the place where the actual change is taking place. Often this conflict remains long after the change has taken place.

The three situations are only slected examples, each unique in itself. At the same time, each is typical in the sense that such complex situations are to be found throughout those parts of the Detroit system where the different forces of change are operating. As has been seen, much of the Detroit metropolitan area is involved. In the mid-1970s these situations pervade and typify every zone of the spatial model described above. In a real sense, they are the very essence of the Detroit system.

Conclusion

A number of basic themes pervade this study. Among them, perhaps the most basic is the theme of diversity. The vast sprawling entity that we call the Detroit system incorporates a rich and varied mosaic of areas, landscapes, and peoples. Clearly this is one of the system's great assets. Diversity has contributed greatly to the remarkable past achievements of the Detroit system. It provides an underlying color and vitality that sometimes is hidden beneath the surface monotony found in much of the area. It is one of the system's sources of promise for the future.

At the same time diversity has its dangers. These occur when diversity leads to differentiation and segregation, a second theme which pervades this study. In its development, the Detroit system has been differentiated into a set of different social areas. Although this differentiation occurs at a number of levels, attention in this study has focused upon the six zones of the spatial model discussed earlier. In many respects the zones constitute different "realms," which are separated by social distance and by different mental and perceptual outlooks. Among those different outlooks, probably the most important is the perception that persons in each zone have of the remainder of the Detroit system. With the passage of time the segregation of these different realms has become more pronounced. This has been accentuated by the spatial expansion of the whole system, which has increased the scope of the different realms.

Persons in one realm can become "locked in" to the activities of their own social world, and come to know and care less and less about other realms. Ignorance of the Detroit zones on the part of the two suburban zones appears to increase as time passes and as the spatial extent of those suburban zones expands. Meanwhile, the lack of knowledge about the outlying zones shown by residents of the Inner Zone continues to increase. In sum, social differentiation, and its accompanying liabilities, tend to become self-perpetuating.

The increasing differentiation of the Detroit system's social realms appears to contradict another theme of this study—namely, the continuing interdependence of different parts of the system. Each zone of our spatial model plays an essential functional role within the total system. That role has its economic aspects. For example, decisionmaking tends to take place in the Suburban Area of Radial Development, whereas much of the skilled technical work force is provided by the Suburban Area of Intersectoral Development. The role played by each zone also has its social aspects. The Inner Zone, for example, has become a haven for publicly supported institutions, and also the receptacle for much that is unwanted or prohibited elsewhere in the system. By contrast, the Zone of Rural Change still provides the breathing space, or the "release force," of the system, giving the feeling that there is still somewhere to go when conditions elsewhere become too unpleasant.

In spite of increasing segregation, the Detroit system still is a functioning entity; it is a system in the most basic sense of the word.

Another dominant theme is that of change. In this study, emphasis has been put upon the broad forces of change that engulf and transform different parts of the system. Such forces are not only disruptive in themselves, they bring instability in advance, and often leave blight in their wake. Virtually every force of change that has been discussed in this study has been responsible for some degree of deterioration, whether in terms of direct destruction, or in terms of "limbo" associated with delay and uncertainty. In aggregate, much of the Detroit system shows the adverse effects of these forces of change.

Even a cursory examination of these forces of change points up another theme of this study—that of complexity. In trying to piece together what is happening in Oakland Township, in northwest Detroit, and in the Cass Corridor, the authors were confronted with such a complex of interrelated elements and events that it was impossible to account for all of them and difficult to put them into perspective. At a larger scale, those complexities become magnified.

When the basic and often contradictory themes woven through this vignette are looked at in perspective, the resulting picture indicates a fundamental dichotomy. On the one hand, all themes bring out elements of strength in the Detroit system. The rich diversity of its landscapes and peoples is one of the system's strongest assets. Even the changes that engulf the system are elements of strength in that change brings about freshness, new outlooks, original adaptations, and the proof of resiliency of areas. These strengths have been present throughout the Detroit system's history and still are evident today.

On the other hand, all of the themes bring out elements of weakness. Diversity can mean the preservation of exclusiveness, and can lead to segregation. Change, no matter how refreshing, also brings about the instability and deterioration that have been amply depicted in these pages. The fundamental dichotomy suggested here is one of the clear impressions to emerge from this study.

Much of the future of the Detroit system depends upon whether the system can capitalize upon the strengths inherent in the themes presented here, or whether it becomes overwhelmed by their weaknesses. If the system can harness the strength, vitality, freshness, and productive capacity of the diverse elements in its makeup, then it has a sound future. However, if the system cannot control and reverse the inherent weaknesses expressed here, its future is less promising. Thus, diversity is a source of strength and should be cherished, but it should not be allowed to lead to the stifling differentiation that often has characterized the past. Forces of change should be welcomed, but they should be prevented from bringing the legacy of instability and deterioration that has been described in this study.

In the immediate future the unfavorable side of the dichotomy appears to have the upper hand. Indeed the weakness inherent in the themes presented in these pages has much to do with the negative image that Detroit presents in the midseventies. As this study is brought to a conclusion, this image is accentuated by a worsening economic climate of the system's industrial base. In the longer term, the prospect might not be so pessimistic. The system includes a population of five million productive people, a rich variety of ethnic and socio-economic groups, a vigorous black community, a strong industrial structure, and a history of impressive achievements. Today there is some optimism in such diverse examples as the well-publicized Renaissance Center and Fairlane developments, the increased strength of local community councils throughout the metropolitan area, and a new City of Detroit Charter which attempts to remedy past inequities. If these and other developments have some meaning, and if the more favorable side of the dichotomy presented here reasserts itself, the Detroit system would change its present negative image and regain a leadership role which has been characteristic of much of its past.

Bibliography

Atlas and Plat Book of Oakland Township, Michigan, 1956, 1967, and *1973.* Rockford, Ill.: Rockford Map Publishing Co., 1956, 1967, and 1973.

Boyer, Brian D. *Cities Destroyed for Cash: The FHA Scandal at HUD.* Chicago, Ill.: Follett, 1973.

Bunge, William. *Fitzgerald: Geography of a Revolution.* Cambridge, Mass.: Schenkman, 1971.

City of Detroit. *Commercial Land Utilization Study, Volumes I and II.* Detroit, 1974.

City of Detroit, Community Development Commission. Urban Renewal Planning Office. Miscellaneous Statistics.

City of Detroit, Community Renewal Program. *Detroit: The New City.* Detroit, 1966.

——. University City Urban Renewal Project, 1960.

City of Detroit, Police Department Records..

Deskins, Donald. R., Jr. *Residential Mobility of Negroes in Detroit, 1837-1965.* Ann Arbor, Mich.: University of Michigan, Department of Geography, Michigan Geographical Publication no. 5, 1970.

Detroit Free Press, September 17, 1972, and March 17, 1973.

Detroit Model Neighborhood Agency. *Detroit Model Neighborhood Household Survey – Statistical Tables, Summer of 1972.* Detroit, 1972.

Doxiadis, Constantinos A. *Emergence and Growth of an Urban Region: The Developing Urban Detroit Area.* Vols. I, II and III. Detroit:

Detroit Edison Company, Wayne State University–Doxiadis Associates, 1966.

Hartman, David W. "From 'Piety Hill' to 'Slum Alley': A Social Analysis of the Schoolcraft Community," Ph.D. Dissertation, Wayne State University, 1975.

Katzman, David M. *Before the Ghetto: Black Detroit in the Nineteenth Century.* Urbana, Ill.: University of Illinois Press, 1973.

Michigan State Housing Development Authority. *Consideration for a Housing Strategy for the City of Detroit.* Report prepared by the American City Corporation for the Michigan State Housing Development Authority. Detroit, 1973.

National Council for Geographic Education. *Metropolitan America: Geographic Perspectives and Teaching Strategies.* The 1972 NCGE Yearbook. Oak Park, Ill., 1972.

Northwest Community Organization (Organization for Citizens Community Councils for Northwest Detroit). Miscellaneous Information.

Oakland Township Association (Oakland Township, Michigan). Miscellaneous Information.

Parkins, Almon E. *The Historical Geography of Detroit.* Lansing, Mich.: Michigan Historical Commission, 1918.

Peoples Area Development Corporation. *A Physical Development Program for PADCO.* Report prepared by William Kessler and Associates, Inc., and Lucas and Edwards, Inc. Detroit, 1973.

Sinclair, Robert. *The Face of Detroit: A*

Spatial Synthesis. Detroit: Wayne State University–National Council for Geographic Education–U.S. Office of Education, 1970.

Sinclair, Robert. "Ghetto Expansion and the Urban Landscape," *Wiener Geographische Schriften, Festschrift Leopold G. Scheidl* vol. 2 (1975).

Smith, William D. *Community Development in the Wayne Area.* Detroit: Center for Urban Studies, Wayne State University, 1970.

Southeast Michigan Council of Governments. Planning and Research Division. Detroit, Michigan. Miscellaneous Statistics and Information.

———. *1974 Residential Construction in Southeast Michigan.* Detroit, 1974.

State of Michigan, Department of State Highways and Transportation. Miscellaneous Statistics.

Sales Management Magazine: 1974 Survey of Buying Power. As quoted in the *Oakland Press,* January 25, 1975.

The *Community Reporter* (Detroit), September 24, 1969, and April 8, 1970.

The Detroit News, March 15, 1973.

Thompson, Bryan. Detroit Area Ethnic Groups, 1971. Map. Wayne State University–Detroit Public Schools TTT Project, 1972.

Transportation and Land Use Study. *A Profile of Southeastern Michigan. Talus Data, 1965.* Detroit, 1968.

United Northwest Detroit Real Estate Association. Multilist of Houses for Sale, February 1973.

U.S. Bureau of the Census. *Census of Population and Housing; 1970 Census Tracts.* Final Report PHC (1)-58 Detroit, Michigan SMSA.

U.S. Bureau of the Census. *Census of Population; 1970. Detailed Characteristics.* Final Report PC (1)-D24 Michigan.

U.S. Bureau of the Census. *Census of Population: 1970. General Economic and Social Characteristics.* Final Report PC (1)-C24 Michigan.

U.S. Bureau of the Census. Miscellaneous publications.

U.S. Department of Housing and Urban Development. Detroit Office Files.

Widick, B.J. *Detroit: City of Race and Class Violence.* Chicago, Ill.: Quadrangle Books, 1972.

Wolf, Eleanor P., and Lebeaux, Charles N. *Change and Renewal in an Urban Community. Five Case Studies of Detroit* New York: Praeger, 1969.

Information for the Cass Corridor, Northwest Detroit, and Oakland Township Case studies was supplemented by field research during the year 1973. Field work included field mapping, structured questionnaires, and informal interviews.

About the Authors

Robert Sinclair is a graduate of Wayne State University. His graduate work was done at Northwestern University where he received his Ph.D. degree in 1955. Dr. Sinclair has been awarded three Fulbright grants, the most recent in Austria for the academic year 1976–'77. His research interests are in economic geography, especially land use theory and problems associated with urban and urban fringe areas, and the geography of Europe. Dr. Sinclair is Professor of Geography at Wayne State University, Detroit, Michigan.

Bryan Thompson is a graduate of the University of Toronto. He did his graduate work at Clark University and was awarded a Ph.D. degree in 1971. His research interests are primarily in urban geography with special emphasis on the nature of neighborhood change, and the urban experiences of immigrants arriving in America after 1850. Dr. Thompson is Associate Professor of Geography at Wayne State University, Detroit, Michigan.

Metropolitan Detroit:
An Anatomy
of Social Change

Association of American Geographers

Comparative Metropolitan Analysis Project

Vol. 1   Contemporary Metropolitan America: Twenty Geographical Vignettes. Cambridge: Ballinger Publishing Company, 1976.

Vol. 2.   Urban Policymaking and Metropolitan Dynamics: A Comparative Geographical Analysis. Cambridge: Ballinger Publishing Company, 1976.

Vol. 3.   A Comparative Atlas of America's Great Cities: Twenty Metropolitan Regions. Minneapolis: University of Minnesota Press, 1976.

Vignettes of the following metropolitan regions are also published by Ballinger Publishing Company as separate monographs:

- Boston
- New York-New Jersey
- Philadelphia
- Hartford-Central Connecticut
- Baltimore
- New Orleans
- Atlanta
- Chicago
- St. Paul-Minneapolis
- Seattle
- Miami
- Los Angeles
- Detroit

Supported by a grant from the National Science Foundation.